W9-AHD-904

NATIVE AMERICAN FAITH *in* AMERICA

MICHAEL GARRETT AND J.T. GARRETT

J. GORDON MELTON, SERIES EDITOR

®

Facts On File, Inc.

NATIVE AMERICAN FAITH IN AMERICA

Faith in America

The producers thank writers Johnny Flynn and Jean Kinney Williams for their contributions
to the preparation of this book

Facts On File, Inc.

132 West 31st Street

New York NY 10001

Library of Congress Cataloging-in-Publication Data

Garrett, Michael Tlanusta, 1970-

     Native American faith in America / Michael Garrett and J.T. Garrett.

         p. cm.—(Faith in America)

     Includes bibliographical references and index.

     ISBN 0-8160-4989-0 (hardcover)

      1. Indians of North America—Religion. 2. Indians of North America—Social life and customs.

        3. United States—Religious life and customs. I. Title. II. Series.

     E98.R3G37 2003

     299'.793—dc21   2002156384

Produced by the Shoreline Publishing Group LLC

Editorial Director: James Buckley Jr.

Contributing Editor: Beth Adelman

Designed by Thomas Carling, Carling Design, Inc.

Photo research by Laurie Schuh

Index by Nanette Cardon, IRIS

Photo and art credits: Cover: AP/Wide World (main image, top right); North Wind Archives (middle right);
Anne Scheuerman (bottom right). Interior: AP/Wide World 6, 47, 50, 52, 61, 63, 74, 77, 85, 88, 93, 95, 110, 117;
Bridgeman Art Archives 19, 25, 68; Corbis 13, 71, 96, 101, 106; Getty Images 112; North Wind Archives 27, 32, 45,
79, 82; Philbrook Museum of Art 16, 21, 36, 40; Anne Scheuerman 98; Courtesy Sports Immortals, Inc. 59

Printed in the United States of America

VB 10 9 8 7 6 5 4 3 2 1

This book is printed on acid-free paper.

CONTENTS

Foreword by J. Gordon Melton   4

INTRODUCTION   Native American Beliefs and Practices   7

CHAPTER 1   The Coming of the Long Knives   25

CHAPTER 2   Key Events in Native American History   41

CHAPTER 3   From Moccasins to Music: Cultural Influences   53

CHAPTER 4   Native American Faith and Society   67

CHAPTER 5   American Politics and Native Americans   81

CHAPTER 6   Important Native American Leaders   95

CHAPTER 7   Winds of Change Blow Across the Land   113

Glossary   120

Time Line   122

Resources   123

Index   124

FOREWORD

AMERICA BEGINS A NEW MILLENNIUM AS ONE OF THE MOST RELIGIOUSLY diverse nations of all time. Nowhere else in the world do so many people—offered a choice free from government influence—identify with such a wide range of religious and spiritual communities. Nowhere else has the human search for meaning been so varied. In America today, there are communities and centers for worship representing all of the world's religions.

The American landscape is dotted with churches, temples, synagogues, and mosques. Zen Buddhist zendos sit next to Pentecostal tabernacles. Hasidic Jews walk the streets with Hindu swamis. Most amazing of all, relatively little conflict has occurred among religions in America. This fact, combined with a high level of tolerance of one another's beliefs and practices, has let America produce people of goodwill ready to try to resolve any tensions that might emerge.

The Faith in America series celebrates America's diverse religious heritage. People of faith and ideals who longed for a better world have created a unique society where freedom of religious expression is a keynote of culture. The freedom that America offers to people of faith means that not only have ancient religions found a home here, but that newer forms of expressing spirituality have also taken root. From huge churches in large cities to small spiritual communities in towns and villages, faith in America has never been stronger. The paths that different religions have taken through American history is just one of the stories readers will find in this series.

Like anything people create, religion is far from perfect. However, its contribution to the culture and its ability to help people are impressive, and these accomplishments will be found in all the books in the series. Meanwhile, awareness and tolerance of the different paths our neighbors take to the spiritual life has become an increasingly important part of citizenship in America.

Today, more than ever, America as a whole puts its faith in freedom—the freedom to believe.

Native American Faith in America

No segment of American religious life embodies as much diversity as that which exists within the Native American world. Most of the more than 500 Native American nations continue to exist as the 21st century begins, each with its own language and unique spiritual traditions. While several themes run through the spirituality that underlies a large number of Native American cultures, the religious beliefs and practices vary considerably, especially among groups originating in geographically separated parts of the country.

Added to the traditional spiritual life of Native Americans has been the widespread acceptance of Christianity in response to massive efforts of various churches (from Roman Catholic to Mormon) to integrate Native Americans into their fellowships. While often criticized for their use of secular pressure to increase Native conversions to Christianity and to force them to accept white European culture, Christianity continues to have an immense appeal within the Native community. In the last generation Native Americans have wielded this influence to demand changes and accommodation from the various churches that have significant Native membership.

In the contemporary world, many Native Americans straddle two worlds, holding membership in tribal groups, some of which have the status of separate nations, but at the same time being American citizens. As such, their role in developing American culture has been immense. Native Americans now experience a new acceptance among Americans who wish to learn from Native spirituality—an acceptance that many feel may actually threaten their attempt to revive and preserve their fragile heritage. *Native American Faith in America* attempts to make sense of this complex religious world, still largely unknown to most Americans.

— J. Gordon Melton, Series Editor

INTRODUCTION

Native American Beliefs and Practices

"There is this world in which we live, but there is also one above us and one below us. . . Here where we live is the center of our world."
— Maria Solares, or Qililkutayiwit, a Chumash mythologist (1842?–1923)

WHEN EUROPEANS FIRST CAME TO THE LAND THAT WOULD BE CALLED America, there were more than 600 tribes of people—Native Americans—living in North America. Each tribe had its own language, territory, and religious beliefs and practices. The specifics of Native American beliefs, traditions, and rituals were and are as varied as the number of tribes who lived and still live in North America. However, some central themes are shared by most tribes and will appear throughout this book. Among these are the importance of the land to Native Americans; their identity as individual tribes first and as members of the larger group of Native Americans second; and their understanding of their place in the cosmos as "The People," created specially by a Creator to live in a specific place. All of these beliefs were challenged as their world changed forever with the coming of the Europeans.

The spiritual life of Native Americans was most drastically affected by the Christian religion the Europeans brought with them. As we will show in coming chapters, the impact of Christian evangelists (people who spread the

Throughout this book, we will use the term Native American to refer to the people who were living in the Americas at the time of Columbus, or who are descended from those people. The term "Indian" may be used when quoting other sources or in the names of organizations such as the Bureau of Indian Affairs. The two terms refer to the same group of people.

However, just as Asian Americans think of themselves as first and foremost people from specific Asian countries, all Native Americans are, in their own minds, members of their individual tribes. Names of those tribes will be used when referring to specific events or people, as necessary.

PRECEDING PAGE
Traditional dance
A woman dances at a 2001 powwow in Virginia. These large gatherings have been held more frequently in recent years as Native Americans from many tribes rediscover their traditional practices and beliefs.

Gospel) was deep and varied. Some Native Americans underwent forced conversion, while others enjoyed education provided by missionaries. As with most things, there were good and bad aspects to this evangelization. Whatever the effect of Christianity on times past, the result today is that most Native Americans who profess a specific religion are members of Christian denominations.

Unlike African Americans, however, Native Americans have generally not set up their own separate Christian groups, but have joined existing churches, from Catholic to Baptist to Pentecostal and other Protestant denominations. For many years, their impact on those groups was almost nonexistent. In recent years, however, changing attitudes toward diversity have enabled them to have some small influence on ceremonies and rituals, such as including Native dancers in a Catholic Mass or using Native American worship music in other Christian services.

In addition, thanks in part to a renewed sense of community inspired by 1960s political activism (see chapter 5), many Native Americans are finding ways to rediscover their roots. Young people are working to revive and continue millennia-old traditions, rituals, and ceremonies. Spiritually based dances, such as the Sun Dance (see page 17), are becoming more popular. Through literature, film, and television, Native Americans are exploring their heritage.

The key to understanding how this mix operates today, whether within or outside a Christian context, is to understand the roots of the deeply-felt beliefs held by Native Americans yesterday and today. This introductory chapter will try to sum up some of the general principles of Native American beliefs, keeping in mind the immense diversity of traditions held by the many different tribes across North America.

The Creation

How long these people we call Native Americans have lived on the opposite side of the world from Europe is a matter of dispute. Some scientists believe the Indians, as explorer Christopher Columbus (1451–1506) named the people he encountered, came into the Americas from the northwest by using an ancient land bridge across the Bering Strait, between what is today northwest Russia and the western tip of Alaska. However, Native Americans, as the first people of the Americas are now called, have no stories, written or remembered, of such a journey. (More details on this theory are in chapter 1.)

Some Native American creation stories say they came into their land by climbing up from the world or worlds below. Others believe they traveled to this Middle World in a journey to find the exact place where they were supposed to live. Sometimes the beings of the sky, sun, moon, or stars, guided the First People to the Center of the World, as in the Zuni concept of their homeland. In other cases, the plants or animals of the Middle World led the First People to the place where they were to live and flourish. Each of the tribes in North America have their own story about where they came from and why they chose to settle where they were at the time the Europeans arrived.

Most Native American nations have no word in their language for the European concepts of "religion," "Indian," or "Native American." Instead, they have a concept of themselves as The People, as distinct from the First Animals, who were people in the Before Time. The Before Time was a sacred time, when animals were the first beings to live on the earth. The animals planned what the First People would look like, how these new creatures called humans would live, and maybe even where they would live. In that sense, every living thing in the world is related to human beings.

Not a Typical Religion

When most people think of religion, they picture a church, a synagogue, or a mosque. There were tribal groups in North America in times past who built temples made of earth or stone, but for the most part it is the natural world where tribes prayed and made sacrifices to their concept of the Supreme Being. For Native peoples today, their place of worship might be a mountaintop, a spring, or a small sweatlodge in a canyon deep in the woods as easily as a church.

Such a diversity of people spawned a wide array of ideas about what constitutes a religion and how religious ideas are expressed. People have often referred to the Native American concept of the sacred or the holy as the Great Spirit, and it is true that many Native American people believe in a single creator. But in some cases Native American people believe that the creator or creators are both male and female. Some tribes believe that a feminine spirit was responsible for the creation of the world and humans. Others believe in a gender-neutral creator—that is, a creator who is neither male nor female but has the power to create the world and all that is in it.

SWEATLODGE
The sweatlodge is a hut or enclosed area in which stones are heated so hot that when water is poured over them, it turns into steam. As those inside the sweatlodge perspire, they undergo a spiritual purification and cleansing, preparing them for an upcoming ritual. The sweatlodge still is used today as a purification rite among several North American Native peoples.

A Creation Story

Throughout the forests of Canada and the northern United States, where the weather did not encourage farming, were hunting and gathering tribes such as the Cree, the Ojibwa, and the Algonquin. Here is a creation story from the Algonquin, which appears in *North American Indian Mythology* (1985) by Cottie Burland.

The creator spirit was named Gluskap, and he had a destructive wolf-brother named Malsum. From the body of the Earth Mother, Gluskap made the plants, animals, people, and their landscape. From Malsum came thorny thickets, rocks, and poisonous animals.

Malsum attempted to kill Gluskap with an owl feather, the only thing that could harm him. Gluskap did die when pierced by the feather, but his powers were also great enough that he could bring himself back to life. He then sought out his brother and killed Malsum with the only thing he was susceptible to: the root of a fern. Malsum's evil powers went underground and he turned into a vicious wolf.

Gluskap could now finish the creation of the world. Once, he was approached by four beggars who each had a different request. Gluskap granted all four of them their wishes, but not as they all had expected. The fourth man, who wanted to be taller than other men so he could rule over them, was turned into an enormous pine tree which was, indeed, taller than any man.

Gluskap finally met his match in a surprising way, which taught him a lesson about being too proud of his powers and accomplishments. One day a poor old woman told him she knew of someone, inside her small bark hut, with whom his authority would make no difference. He didn't believe her as he entered her hut, where a baby was sitting on the floor. Gluskap first sang to the baby, and received a big smile in return. He then commanded the baby to walk, but it was too young and couldn't understand him, and just continued to smile. Gluskap entertained the baby, who laughed, but couldn't speak when Gluskap commanded him to. An angry Gluskap finally had to face the fact he'd been defeated. After a while, he left the land of the Algonquins in his canoe, paddling toward the sunrise, but he might return some day.

At the heart of the Lakota religion was and is the Wakan Tanka, the term that represents the mysterious supernatural force that permeates everything in existence. The term can be translated as Great Mysterious or Incomprehensibility, and Wakan also can be compared to the word "holy." The Wakan Tanka are those who made everything, and while there are many of them, all are really one spirit.

The Crow believe in a supreme being whose name translates to Starter of All Things or First Worker. He did not have a physical body, but was made up of the misty elements that existed before he made the world. First Worker, they believe, created all life and objects on the earth, and the Crow pray to him during their Sun Dance ceremony (see page 17).

For the Pawnee, Tirawahat is the supreme being who is present in all things, especially thunderstorms. Included in their beliefs is the idea that the gods leave the earth in winter; spring's first thunder means they have returned and a series of ceremonies begins. The first thunder is the voice of Paruksti, a divine messenger from Tirawahat, and as the gods return, so life is rekindled. In their ceremonies, they give thanks for the new life—animals, crops, and return of the buffalo— that comes each spring.

The Spirit and the Natural World

The cultures and religions of Native Americans are greatly influenced by their surroundings, and their beliefs and spiritual practices reflect the variety of those natural settings. The tribes today maintain similar traditions, first started by their ancestors.

The Native peoples who lived in the Southwest, called the Pueblos by the Spanish because of the villages they established, were at first primarily farmers. Water and rainfall were precious, and so much of the religion of these Hopi and Zuni people, among other groups, was focused on prayers for rain.

Those people who lived in the near-arctic regions remained nomadic hunters. The harshness of their environment, with its terrible winter storms and less abundant food supply, made them often appear to be equally harsh, at least to outsiders. Because both humans and animals had to kill to survive, the Inuit people of the far north assumed the powerful animals they hunted, such as the polar bear, had powerful spirits, too.

The people who settled in the Pacific Northwest, on the other hand, had abundant resources, unlike the peoples to their north and south. Game from the sea and the forests was plentiful, and the forest provided wood for building their homes as well as the impressive canoes, holding up to 40 men, that they dug out from trunks of trees. Their life of plenty was reflected in their more materially advanced culture, such as their well-crafted woodwork, and large villages (up to 1,000 people), which usually were located at the mouths of rivers, making transportation to other villages relatively simple. The Northwest coastal tribes had such a wealth of natural resources that their religion included ceremonies designed to curb greediness, a human tendency they believed would be displeasing to the spirits they looked to for help and guidance.

Not surprisingly, there were many legends about buffalo spirits among the Plains Native Americans. When food was scarce, prayers were offered to the Earth Mother, who guarded the buffalo spirits underground, and she was asked to supply more buffalo for the people.

One of the most important figures in the Sioux religion is White Buffalo Woman, a Wakan Tanka who first brought the very important pipe to the Lakota people. White Buffalo Woman was a lovely, heavenly maiden. One day, two Lakota men were hunting and climbed a high spot to search for game. They saw a beautiful young woman dressed in white buckskin walking toward them. One of the men thought her to be holy, while the other young man saw her quite differently, and felt lustful. When she stood before them, she recognized the desirous look of the one man and he was destroyed. To the other she gave a pipe, which was sacred, and she told him to use it as he walked the earth, because the earth is also sacred.

Totem Masks and Poles

One of the ideas that can be found among many tribes in North America is the totem. The word *totem* is from the Algonquin language, and it means an animal, plant, or natural power that serves as the direct ancestor of a clan.

Within a single tribal group there might be a number of clans. Clans might be named after the powers of the sky, such as thunder, sun, winds, or rain, or the power of birds, plants, or animals. The members of the clan sometimes carve a mask or a small figure to depict the attributes of their clan. Some tribes in the far northwest of America may carve an entire tree, called a totem pole, to depict the history of their clan. Other clans or individuals keep a piece of fur, feather, claw, tooth, or some other part of the animal that represents their clan ancestor. While not every tribe has a system of clans, individual names could also be given honoring the powers of the animal or plant world, the sky or the weather.

Henceforth, the pipe has been used in prayer, its tobacco smoke carrying the prayers and thoughts of those smoking it to the Great Spirit. All aspects of the pipe are symbolic: the bowl represents the earth, the wooden stem represents all living things. Animals are carved into pipe bowls, and feathers are often hung from it.

Smoking the pipe was, and is, a principal part of religious worship for the Sioux. It is also smoked to show that a conflict between enemies has ended (as in a "peace pipe"), or to unite tribes or individuals as friends.

The Influence and Role of Animals

Animals are also important in the lives and beliefs of Native Americans. They generally do not consider themselves superior to animals, but believe the animals' role in the world as a resource for people—meat, skins, or bone for tools—is something the animals, at some point, voluntarily chose to perform. In fact, in many Native American religions, animals play an important part in the creation of people, and usually have human traits such as speech, or virtues such as bravery or generosity.

One story found among various tribes, such as the Blackfoot tribe from the Plains, tells of a few animals floating on water aboard a raft or a log before the world was created. One of them, sometimes a turtle or a water beetle, dived into the water, scooped some mud from the bottom of the sea, and brought it back up to form the first dry land.

The Menomini tribe from Wisconsin believes that the first human beings came from bears. Two bears, a male and a female, came out of the earth at the mouth of the Menomini River, and they then turned into the first man and woman.

The eagle also is admired among tribes from one coast to the other. The Cherokee hold an Eagle Dance that is a tribute to the great bird of prey's power and strength. In an Apache story from the Southwest, Eagle killed a horrible monster that had been killing people. A mythological bird of prey, the Thunderbird, appears in stories from different parts of the country.

Some Native stories teach that fire came to them because the first coyote stole fire from the sun for humans. Others believe basket weaving was a gift from Grandmother Spider, or wood-carving was a skill taught by an ancestor of the beavers. Whatever the belief system individual tribes have, it is deeply rooted in the natural world. Animals, plants, rivers, lakes, mountains, and springs are all incorporated into a system of belief that can be called Sacred Geography. But just as the high plains in the middle of North America are different from the Rocky Mountains, so too the culture of the Pawnee Indians is different from that of the Arapahoe.

Ceremonies and Rituals

While every tribe is and was different, each has important rituals and ceremonies that helped bring the tribe together to advance common goals. Here are some examples of some of those events.

Corn was the most important crop for the Cherokee, and much mythology developed about it. For example, the first woman, Selu (pronounced *Shay-loo*, it means "first corn,") came from a corn stalk. She kept some ears of corn to remind her of her beginnings, but she did not realize the corn was food until she saw a wild turkey nibbling at it. Later, she voluntarily died for her twin sons, but warned them that they must follow certain procedures to ensure and honor each year's corn crop, or she would send them misfortune.

And so the highlight of the Cherokee's many festivals during the year is Itse Selu, or the Green Corn Festival, celebrated in September as the first ears of corn ripen. The four-day festival originally marked the beginning of the new year and also was a thanksgiving feast.

Itse Selu was also a time of cleansing—bathing in a river, perhaps wearing new clothes, or sweeping out the family's home. The old corn from the last harvest was finished up, and no new corn could be eaten before the festival began. Old grudges were forgiven. Most important, each home's hearth fire, which had been kept burning since

The Role of Shamans

Shamans were important figures among tribes throughout Native America. Their role often was as a healer, since illness was generally thought to be caused by a person being out of sync with the controlling spiritual powers. If that situation was not made right, it was feared that the person's spiritual imbalance, in the form of physical illness, would affect other tribe members, too.

Sometimes the shaman would go into a trance, slipping out of consciousness, in order to visit the spirit world and re-adjust the ill person's relationship with those forces.

Among some tribes the shaman was more of a prophet, who could help direct the people in their actions because of his ability to make contact with the spirit world. The Navajo shamans in the Southwest held ceremonies in which they interceded between people and spirits with a variety of rituals. One such ritual was sand painting. An elaborate image was made by carefully pouring colored sand on the ground. The image was hoped to be pleasing to the spirits. At the end of the ceremony, the sand painting was erased. Buddhist monks use a similar sort of sand painting, called a mandala, that is carefully made then erased.

The shaman did not preach to clan or tribe members, whose religious instruction began in childhood. Rather, the shaman performed a service—that of helping other tribe members connect with the spirit world.

the previous Itse Selu, was put out. Then the village was ready for an important ritual—the start of the next fire. A priest rubbed sticks together to begin a new fire, which would burn for the upcoming year in a village temple. From that fire came the hot embers that would start the new hearth fires in each village household.

Much dancing, story telling, and feasting on corn, beans, and hunted game made Itse Selu a very anticipated festival. Putting the old year behind and starting the new one with a clean hearth and a thankful heart helped maintain the balance necessary to sustain life. The Green Corn Festival is still celebrated in some fashion in many Cherokee families and tribes.

Corn was also an extremely important crop to the Hopi, and they believed prayer was most influential in bringing about a fruitful harvest. In their many religious ceremonies they prayed for rain, a long and

Sun Dance
This 1946 painting by Archie Blackowl, titled Sunrise Dance of the Sun Dance, *depicts a version of the ceremony as performed by members of the Cheyenne Nation.*

healthy life, and fertility. One of the most important prayer ceremonies was the Soyalangw, which occurred at the winter solstice in December. Its rituals were concerned with fertility and the approaching planting season. Soyalangw was carried out by the highest ranking manhood society, although there were other religious societies for both men and women.

The Sun Dance

Group ceremonies were effective in pulling a tribe together and instilling unity and pride, and they remain a source of strength for Native groups today. Perhaps the most powerful group ceremony the Plains tribes performed was the Sun Dance, a form of which is still done today. According to the 1994 book *Native American Myths and Legends* (edited by Colin Taylor), today's Sun Dance was derived from a ritual called O-kee-pa, practiced by the Mandan tribe, which was almost wiped out by smallpox in the 1830s.

The Sun Dance originally occurred around the summer solstice, in connection with the big buffalo hunt. As in the older O-kee-pa ritual, at the center of the Sun Dance were young men who went through a tortuous episode of being hung from a tree-trunk pole by splints, which cut through their chest or back muscles. It was seen as the ultimate offering to the Sun (a father figure), much more significant than a food or animal offering.

The offering was made to ask for protection over the whole tribe, and the men who went through the painful and bloody ordeal were admired for their courage and looked to as future leaders of the tribe.

Some men went through the hardship of the Sun Dance to show gratitude to the Great Spirit for having been spared in battle. They were grateful not because they had been afraid to die, but because their families would have experienced much sadness in losing a loved one.

In the 1880s, the United States government banned the Sun Dance, considering it to be barbaric, but it remained an important ritual performed secretly for many years by tribes of the northern plains in hidden away places such as the Badlands in South Dakota. In the 20th century, Native Americans won the right to practice their tribal religions (see page 86), and the Sun Dance underwent a more formal reintroduction among Plains tribes. Some still practice it today, although without some of the more painful aspects of the past rituals.

The Passages of Life

As with all other aspects of their spiritual life, different Native American groups have different ceremonies and traditions associated with the important milestones of life. For example, the Hopi see corn as a life-sustaining gift that comes about from the joint efforts of a motherly earth and a fatherly sky (in the form of rain). So linked is corn with life itself that a newborn Hopi baby is kept indoors, away from sunlight, for 20 days, just as corn planted takes about 10 days to sprout and then requires another 10 days of protection from the sun. A Hopi baby is named on its 21st day in an outdoor ceremony.

Initiation rites are common among Native American peoples, where children learn the deeper lessons about their tribes' spiritual beliefs and perform various tasks that demonstrate their readiness to take on adult responsibilities.

One such Hopi ceremony is Powamuya, which is also called the Bean Dance. It takes place in February. During several days of ceremony, most of it in the kiva, children aged six through 10 are initiated into the kachina society. They hear from the kachina chief the old stories of the kachinas (special spirits) and how they came from all four directions, bringing crops for the Hopi people. Sand paintings are created, including one featuring a symbol of the sun; that painting is, in part, a prayer for warmth.

Beans are planted in the kivas and then, after they sprout, are distributed to still-uninitiated children at their homes by kachinas. As Powamuya comes to a close, kachinas walk through the village, distributing gifts to children. Finally, the ceremony ends with the Bean Dance at midnight on the ninth day.

Initiated children are brought to the kiva to be let in on a Hopi secret: the kachina figures with which they have interacted during the past week are not actual kachinas, but are the children's relatives acting out the part of the kachinas. The material and the sacred worlds, the children learn, are always interacting. By summer, the kachina "season," or the time when they participate in ceremonies, comes to an end, and the kachinas "leave" until the next Powamuya.

An important ritual for young men of the Plains tribes was the vision quest. In his book *Soul of the Indian*, Charles Eastman compared it to the Christian sacrament of confirmation, where one accepts responsibility for his or her own spiritual direction. Every young man

KIVA

Most Hopi ceremonies take place in kivas, or underground chambers reserved for religious practices. Being underground, the kivas are symbolic of the world the Hopis believe they emerged from, and they enable the Hopi to perform ceremonies in private because, as many Native Americans believe, outside knowledge of the ceremonies would weaken their effectiveness.

KACHINA

There are perhaps as many as 400 kachina spirits, although the exact number is not clear. They represent different natural spirits and are considered prayer messengers, as well as important teachers of children. Kachina spirits are personified through elaborate costumes and masks by dancers in festivals and prayer ceremonies, as well as by dolls.

at puberty left the tribe for a day or up to a few days, and hoped to connect to a spiritual guardian and have a vision or dream that would help guide him throughout his life.

Spirituality was very individualistic among the Sioux; there is no set of religious beliefs to follow, although it was very important to perform a ritual correctly. So it was considered essential for a young man (there are no women's vision quests recorded) to have a powerful spiritual experience to lead him through his life.

Having undergone a vapor bath in a sweatlodge, the young man would seek out a high spot on the landscape, such as a hill or a rocky ledge, where he would spend up to the next four days. He usually wore and brought little with him, and his hair would hang unbraided, all as a sign of humbleness. Facing the sun or the morning star (both of which were believed to wield supernatural power), the man stood or sat without moving for at least 24 hours. He might stay awake all night, praying for a vision, often becoming highly sensitized to his surroundings. Some men became healers after their vision quests, having received the power to do so while in prayer. Some forms of the vision quest are still held today, but are not as elaborate as in years past or as actively practiced. The idea of finding spiritual guidance in solitude is also used by adults, and not just teenagers.

In his book *Black Elk Speaks*, Black Elk (see page 48) described the vision quest of his cousin, Crazy Horse (see page 103). He said Crazy Horse became a chief because as a boy he had a vision that gave him much power. "Crazy Horse dreamed and went into the world where there is nothing but the spirits of all things. That is the real world that is behind this one . . . . He was on his horse in that world, and the horse and himself on it...and everything were made of spirit. . . and everything seemed to float. His horse . . . danced around like a horse made only of shadow, and that is how he got his name, which does not mean that his horse was crazy or wild, but that in his vision it danced around in that queer way." Later, when Crazy Horse was in battle, "he had only to think of that world to be in it again, so that he could go through anything and not be hurt."

In the earlier times, balance was important in all aspects of life for the Cherokee. Men and women maintained separate roles—men hunted and killed in war, while women brought forth new life as mothers and growers of corn or beans. In wedding ceremonies among some southeast tribes, including the Cherokee, the groom's family gave gifts to the bride's family, because the bride was considered to be an asset to the groom. The groom then had to kill a deer or a bear as a symbol of what he would do for his wife during their marriage, while the bride cooked some corn to symbolize what her contributions would be.

Warfare was another example of keeping a balance. It was continuous among the southeast tribes such as the Cherokee, because murders had to be avenged or else a murdered person's soul would be unable to go to the "darkening land" as they were supposed to.

Although these examples of the concept of balance are based on past practices, the idea remains an important part of the Cherokee heritage. Remaining in balance with nature is a key part of this tribe's traditional beliefs.

The Role of Christianity

In terms of faith and belief, Christianity has had the greatest influence on Native Americans. Christian missionaries were among the first

Europeans to arrive in the Americas, and many explorers saw converting the "savage Indians" as a key part of their job. The history of Christian influence on Native Americans is a mixed one, blending care and consideration with outright hostility. Some details of this treatment are included in the following chapters.

Only in recent years have Christian denominations embraced the original spiritual beliefs of Native Americans and begin to include some of those beliefs in the rituals of Christian services. Chumash dancers can be seen performing at Catholic services in California. Native American-designed vestments are worn by priests and ministers in the Southwest. Music influenced by Native American style is used in a variety of Christian services. Theologians and ministers seek ways to combine the message of Jesus with Native American themes, such as in creation stories and in the Christian call for service or humility.

Some individual Christian churches have been more accepting of including traditional activities related to ceremonial practices, especially songs in tribal languages and drums and rattles for song-chants used with funerals and special youth ceremonies. The American Indian Church, located in Garden Grove, California, is one example of a new Christian denomination based on traditional spirituality. It was founded in 1978 to combine Christian teachings with respect for tradition among Native people. Earlier in the 20th century, a church of the Christian sect called the Shakers was established among the Yakimas of Washington State. Missionaries first started the group, but it was soon run by Native Americans themselves, combining traditional spiritual practices with Shaker rites and beliefs.

Some tribes continue to worry about the "outsider" influence of Christian churches. There remain memories of earlier policies that cast aside traditional Native American beliefs and imposed Christian ones (as will be shown in the chapters that follow). However, today there

Native Americans Today

Native Americans today have a steadily growing population of more than 2.4 million people, according to the 2000 U.S. Census. Although this number represents only 1 percent of the total population of the United States, Native people have been described as representing 50 percent of the diversity in our country. Across the United States, there are more than 557 federally recognized and several hundred state-recognized Native American nations.

Given the wide-ranging diversity of this population, it is important, again, to understand that the term "Native American" encompasses the vastness and essence of tribal traditions represented by hundreds of individual nations. Navajo, Catawba, Shoshone, Lumbee, Cheyenne, Cherokee, Apache, Lakota, Seminole, Comanche, Pequot, Cree, Tuscarora, Paiute, Creek, Pueblo, Shawnee, Hopi, Osage, Mohawk, Nez Perce, Seneca—these are but a handful of the hundreds of tribes and nations that still exist today across the United States (a longer list of current and former tribes is on page 31). Native Americans speak approximately 252 different languages (although that number is expected to decrease significantly in the coming years as older Native speakers die).

At the same time, a prevailing sense of "Indianness" based on common worldview and common history seems to bind Native Americans together as a people of many peoples. Maintaining that sense of history and continuing to feel a part of both one's tribe and of the entire Native American population will be a key issue among Native Americans in the future.

is a greater sensitivity to tribal sacred sites, for instance, or to the use of pipe ceremonies and dances. There is also clearly more open-mindedness among the various Christian churches for traditional, spiritual ways. This is especially true in urban areas where there are large numbers of Native Americans, such as Denver, Los Angeles, and New York.

Today, while they continue to keep and hold a variety of Native American spiritual beliefs and customs, many Native Americans are part of a wide variety of Christian denominations. Their relationship to one another is part of the ongoing story of Native American faith.

The Coming of the Long Knives

WHILE THE BEGINNINGS OF EUROPEAN INFLUENCE ON NATIVE American faith and culture can be traced to a specific period of time (the arrival of Europeans, starting in the 15th century), the beginnings of Native culture itself are more mysterious. The theory of most anthropologists and archaeologists is that the ancestors of today's Native Americans arrived on the North American continent via a land bridge from Asia. As long as 50,000 years ago, or as recently as about 15,000 years ago, ice ages created a solid mass connecting Asia and the tip of the Alaskan peninsula. The theory is that Asian peoples followed the game animals across this land bridge and, over a long period of time, spread out across and settled in North America.

This theory is supported by some archaeological evidence, such as carbon-dating of objects found in various parts of what is today the United States and Canada. However, as noted in the introduction, Native Americans' ideas of their origins do not necessarily agree with this theory, and take a more spiritual point of view.

However they got here, the people created an amazingly diverse world. By the 1500s, more than 600 different and separate societies lived in North America. Additional Native tribes and cultures thrived or still survived in Central and South America. Although they did not have a civilization that was recognized by Europeans as being "developed," many of these Native American tribes and nations were highly developed. Some used vast irrigation networks to water their crops. Others developed sophisticated solar calendars. A wide variety of tools, weapons, and ornaments were used by different tribes to hunt, work, cook, and play.

Archaeologists have unearthed evidence of a wide variety of types of societies. The Adena culture, in what is today Ohio, created vast burial mounds for its dead as much as 2,500 years ago. In the Southwest, tribes built large dwellings called pueblos, some of which are still standing in Arizona and New Mexico. About 1,000 years ago, Anasazi people in today's New Mexico built huge buildings that were the largest residences on the continent until the late 1800s. Near present-day St. Louis, the city of Cahokia included dozens of large temples made of wood and animals skins. The Chumash people in California took advantage of the mild weather to spend some of their time in recreation, inventing games and using different musical instruments.

Beyond the physical trappings of society, Native Americans in the time before the Europeans arrived practiced different forms of government. As much as 8,000 years ago, Northwest tribes had created complex social systems with many layers of responsibility among members. More recently, about the year 1000, the Hodenosaunee in the Northeast created a system of law that resembled a modern democracy. Their system became part of the basis for the organizational structure of the Iroquois nation, which would, in turn, inspire Benjamin Franklin and other of America's Founding Fathers (see page 79).

To the south of what would become the United States, other Native cultures were even more sophisticated. The Aztecs, Incas, Maya, Olmec, and other empires covered huge territories. They built enormous temples to their gods, and practiced trade, government, and culture on par with some European societies.

This was the land and these were the people that were suddenly and irrevocably changed when Europeans began arriving in the Americas in the late 15th century. The total population at the point of first contact with Europeans is debated. Some figures are as low as 2 million and as high as 40 million in North America. Including the Central and South American cultures, the number might have been as high as 75 million. Like many aspects of life before Columbus (known among historians as pre-Colombian times), the exact details are a mystery and are the subject of speculation. What is known for certain is that the world these people lived in and the lives they led would soon be gone forever.

The Long Knives Arrive

By far the most significant event in the history of Native American faith and culture was the arrival of waves of Europeans, called "the long knives" by some tribes because of the swords they carried. Coming from Spain, France, Britain, and other countries beginning in the mid-1500s, the new arrivals brought with them the cultures and faiths of their native lands. The greatest impact in the area of faith was felt in the ongoing work of Christian evangelists of many denominations, who tried to convert the Native Americans to Christianity.

Christopher Columbus, although he never visited what would become the United States of America, returned from his travels and inspired almost every European nation to send explorers to various parts of the North and South American continents. They found many

Signs of early times
Petroglyphs, or cave paintings, such as these found in New Mexico, helped archaeologists learn about pre-Colombian Native American culture.

natural wonders, and also discovered that people were already living there. More often than not, the Europeans did not let this stop them from proceeding with exploration and colonization. They also made religious conversion of the native population a major part of their endeavor; in fact, this was the stated mission of the second of Columbus's voyages, and six priests came with him to help.

More often than not, the Native Americans suffered in some way from their encounters with Europeans. Those effects were sometimes sudden and violent, and other times slower-acting but longer-lasting. Throughout the centuries since the first Europeans arrived, the clash and intersection of Native American spiritual values and European ideas and values has been the main focus of Native American life. The events discussed briefly in this chapter focus on the early years of European arrival and their the impact on Native American spirituality and culture. Events noted in chapter 2 focus on key moments of interaction in the 19th and 20th centuries.

The Spanish Arrive

Following Columbus's voyages, which were financed by Spain, several Spanish expeditions headed toward the Americas. The goals of men such as Poncé de Leon (1460–1521), Hernando De Soto (1496?–1542), and Francisco Coronado (1510–1554) were gold and other treasures. Conversion of native populations was not among their aims, and in fact, enslavement or murder was more often the result. Some of their trips took them into Florida, the South, and the Southwest.

After the initial treasure-hunting visits, though, the Catholic Spaniards focused more on conversion. They were partly inspired by Pope Alexander VI (1431–1503), who "gave" the lands of the Americas to Spain to colonize in 1493, with an eye toward converting the native population to Catholicism.

By the early 17th century, Franciscan priests from Spain had established cities in Florida, notably St. Augustine (which has been called the oldest city in the United States). They produced books in some native languages, sometimes having to create the written form of the language themselves because some Native American tribes did not use writing. By 1634, there were more than 30 missions in Florida and they claimed 30,000 converts among the local tribes, which included the Timucuan and Seminole.

MISSION

A mission was a place where missionaries—people who came to the Americas to convert the native population to Christianity—lived and worked. A mission usually included a church, a school, and places for the priests and converts to live. Some also had trading posts and hospitals. Eventually, many of the missions grew into towns.

On the West Coast, Juan Cabrillo (?–1543) sailed from southern California to Oregon in 1542. His experiences there would lead to a major Spanish presence and, eventually, the establishment of a string of missions (see page 30).

The First British Colonies

Seeing the success of the Spanish, the British began to plan for colonies in North America. Although the political and cultural impact of this decision was enormous and long-lasting, we will focus here briefly on its impact on Native spirituality.

Sir Walter Raleigh (1552–1618) was among the first of the British to propose settlements in the New World—as North and South America were called by Europeans. In his petition to Queen Elizabeth I asking for support for his expedition, he used conversion as one of the key arguments. He sent a minister to the New World, Richard Haklyut (1552–1616), with papers saying that the main goal of the voyage would be conversion. The 1970 book by Angie Debo, *A History of the Indians of the United States*, quotes the papers as stating that Raleigh proposed "the gayninge of the soules of millions of those wretched people, the reducing of them from darkness to lighte, from falshoodde to truthe, from dombe [dumb] idolls to the lyvinge God, from the depe pitt of hell to the highest heavens."

The charter later given by King James I to settlers of Jamestown, Virginia, in 1609 asks that colonists bring to the Native people "the true Knowledge and Worship of God." Donations were sent from Britain to the colonists with instructions, according to Debo, to help "bring up the children of infidels . . . in the true knowledge of God and the true Religion." Other donations were sent with the purpose of setting up local schools to teach Native American children English and Anglicanism, the the British Protestant denomination.

In 1620, the Pilgrim community in Plymouth, Massachusetts, was being established with a charter from Charles I that said conversion was one of the "principal endes of this plantation." Among the early missionaries from that community was Thomas Mayhew (1621–1657), a Congregationalist minister and the first governor of Martha's Vineyard, an island off the coast of Massachusetts. He learned the language of the local Pokanoket tribe. Among his early converts was Hiacoomes (c.1610–1690), one of the first Native Americans to become a Christian preacher. After Mayhew was lost at sea on a voyage back to England in 1657, his father, also named Thomas (1593–1682), took up his son's work. Three more generations of Mayhews worked as missionaries to Native Americans in New England.

In 1640, another member of the Massachusetts Bay Colony, John Eliot (1604–1690), began the most formal conversion efforts. Eliot learned the Algonquin language and preached to them. He helped start several schools and churches and was responsible for the first translation of the Bible into a Native American language. He also established what were called "Praying Towns" for Native Americans who had converted to Christianity. These were oases of safety in a time that saw increasingly violent interactions between colonists and indigenous people.

Eliot later expressed disappointment about these violent actions. In Debo's book, Eliot is quoted as saying, "The design of Christ is not to [destroy] nations, but to gospelize them. . . . There is a dark, dark cloud upon the work of the Gospel among the poor Indians."

The cloud grew darker with King Philip's War in 1675, so-called because the Wampanoag leader Metacom (1638–1676) was nicknamed King Philip by the British. Metacom rallied several tribes to attack European settlements in Massachusetts and Connecticut in retaliation for the colonists' continuing encroachment on Native land. Relations did not improve over the ensuing years, and the French and Indian War (1754–1760), which pitted Native Americans and their French allies against British colonial forces, proved to be the end of many Eastern tribes' power.

The Franciscans in the West

The Spanish were the dominant European presence in the West, beginning with the early visits of Cabrillo. In 1769, Franciscan priest Father Junipero Serra (1713–1784), at the direction of King Charles III of Spain, arrived to set up missions. The king wanted to establish permanent settlements in California so that Spain could more firmly control the region. The missionaries built near the coast, where they could establish towns and trade with ships coming to port.

The missionaries introduced Christianity to tribes throughout California and northern Mexico. They forced the Native peoples to live in the missions, an unfamiliar habitat that proved to be unhealthy for the Native population. The first Spanish explorers (as the British would

Native American Tribes

Native Americans divide themselves up into individual tribes, and the tribes join together into nations. This list gives the names of some of the Native American tribes in different geographical regions of the United States before the 1700s. Many of these names will be very familiar to American readers, because the tribe names have been used to name states, geographical features, and even cars. Many of these tribes no longer exist, while others now have just a few members. The 2000 U.S. Census reported a total of 2,475,956 Native Americans living in the United States.

North/Northeast
Abenaki
Algonquin
Conestoga
Delaware
Erie
Fox
Huron
Illinois
Iroquois
Kickapoo
Menominee
Miami
Mohawk
Mohican
Montauk
Narraganset
Ojibway
Oneida
Ottawa
Pawtuxet
Pennacook
Pequot
Potawatomi
Sauk
Seneca
Susqeuhanna
Wampanoag
Winnebago

Southeast
Apalachee
Attacapa
Biloxi
Calusa
Catawba
Cherokee
Chickasaw
Choctaw
Creek
Croatan
Natchez
Powhatan
Quapaw
Saponi
Shawnee
Timucoa
Tuscarora
Tutelo

Plains
Arapaho
Arikara
Brea
Blackfoot
Pawnee
Comanche
Cree
Crow
Iowa
Cheyenne
Nez Perce
Omaha
Osage
Oto
Missouri
Sioux
Ute
Wichita
Caddo Mandan
Shoshone

Southwest
Apache
Cochimi
Hopi
Lagunero
Mohave
Navaho
Paiute
Papago
Pomo
Pueblo
Serrano
Taos
Walapai
Yuma
Zuni

Northwest
Bannock
Chinook
Duwamish
Flathead
Haida
Makah
Nisqualli
Nootka
Paloos
Tenino
Tillamook
Tlingit
Tsimshian
Yakima
Yuki

also do in the East) brought diseases with them to which the Native Americans had never been exposed. Many became ill and died. In fact, by the time the missions were set up, a reduced population of Native Americans found it harder to resist any efforts by the missionaries and their accompanying soldiers. The Native Americans were forced to work on the mission farms raising wheat, corn, and grapes and caring for livestock. They became almost like slaves, and did the majority of the hard labor.

Spreading the word
This idealized mid-19th-century illustration shows a Spanish missionary teaching Native Americans.

The Catholic priests had little or no respect for Native traditions, often finding them barbaric. Most of the Native Americans were baptized and became Christians. They took on the lifestyle and beliefs of the Spanish missionaries, even though both were foreign to them.

Only in recent years has the Catholic Church accepted some responsibility for the devastation caused by these missionaries—some on purpose and some unwittingly. The 21 missions, from San Diego in the south to San Francisco in the north, are all still standing and many are active Catholic parishes.

Dealing with the New United States

The end of the American Revolution in 1781 gave the Native American tribes a new focus: the United States of America. Before then, the tribes were often dealing with French settlers, British colonists, Spanish missionaries and explorers, and others. The establishment of one government over nearly all the territory created a single entity that they could deal with. (There were some areas still under Spanish and French control, but the young United States was already starting to make attempts to include all of that territory. In 1804, for instance, President Thomas Jefferson made the Louisiana Purchase from France, annexing an enormous swath of land west of the Mississippi River.)

From the start, the United States did nothing to encourage much hope among the Native Americans. As the nation grew, settlers pushed further and further westward, displacing tribes and spreading disease. Along with the settlers came more missionaries. The Native Americans began to react more strongly to efforts at conversion. In her 1998 book *A Barren Land: American Indian Dispossession and Survival*, author Paula Mitchell Marks quotes the Seneca leader Red Jacket (1750–1830) as saying in 1792, "We have scarcely a place left to spread our blankets. You have got your country, but you are not satisfied. You want to force your religion on us."

Spiritual leaders such as Tenskawatawa (see page 100) began to speak more forcefully about the rights of Native Americans to their heritage. Other leaders, such as his brother Tecumseh (see page 97) and the Rock Island Sac leader Black Hawk (1767–1837), focused on retaining possession of the Native Americans' land. The new American army fought many battles over the next decades in repeated efforts to drive Native American tribes from land appropriated for the rapidly growing nation.

That land, first west of the Mississippi River and later beginning at a point even further west, was known as Indian Territory. As we will see in this and the next chapter, and in chapter 5, over time that vast land was subsumed into the United States section by section. Treaties were written with Native American tribes that forced them onto reservations, or parcels of land held in trust by the government for the tribe's use. Sadly, though, much of this reservation land was far from the tribe's homelands and often almost uninhabitable. Knowing the deep and spiritual connection that Native Americans had and have to their homeland shows how much of a travesty this reservation policy was.

THE MISSION REVOLT OF 1824

The continuing conflict between Catholic missionaries and the local Native Americans came to head at the Mission La Purisima Concepcion, located north of Santa Barbara, California. In 1824, Spanish soldiers stationed at nearby Mission Santa Iñes beat several local people, and the anger in reaction to this particular beating quickly escalated. It spread to La Purisima and the Chumash people took over that mission for more than a month, holding off soldiers. Eventually, they were defeated and the mission was retaken. It was the most violent of the several clashes between the Spanish missionaries and the Native Americans of California.

Removal: Tricks and Treaties

During the period immediately following the Revolutionary War, the new American government turned most of its attention to acquiring land, adopting a doctrine of discovery and the accompanying sense of entitlement that seemed to be justified by God, race, and sense of place. The United States military was not yet strong enough to take land from Native American tribes by force, and peace with Native tribes was a matter of national security, so the new American government began signing numerous treaties with Native American nations.

The official European-American attitude of the time was that "discovery" of the wilderness areas of North America gave the United States exclusive rights to push Native Americans off their land, either through purchase or conquest. Although initially the American government's intent was peaceful coexistence with Native American nations, including equitable trade relations, greed for land and a rapidly increasing population with the influx of more and more settlers, traders, and fur-trappers, made this goal difficult to maintain.

Although many treaties clearly defined boundaries separating Native American land from United States land, settlers often showed little regard for the boundaries. The American government seldom attempted to keep white intruders off Native American land, and seldom enforced any sort of consequences for those who did intrude.

By 1803, a policy of peaceful coexistence was replaced by an aggressive policy intended to destroy the Native way of life. That year, President Thomas Jefferson was the first to suggest a policy of removal that would include a program to "civilize" Native people through secular and religious education that would transform them into individual farmers who could eventually be integrated into white society. Unfortunately, continued warfare, exposure to European diseases, and the influence of liquor (heretofore unknown among Native Americans) resulted in the rapid disintegration of tribal life for many Native nations.

Through it all, the deep and spiritual connection of Native Americans to the land they were now fighting for—and in most cases losing—was dealt a harsh blow. The aims of the Americans were economic and territorial; the aims of the Native Americans were life and death. This early period from the 1600s to the 1840s can be generally characterized by a saying that was popular among the whites of the time, "The only good Indian is a dead Indian."

General estimates are that about 150 million Native people were killed in the first 400 years following contact with Europeans. By the end of the 18th century, the once-abundant population of Native peoples had been reduced, through warfare and diseases contracted from the invaders, to 10 percent of its original size. This radical decline in population proved disastrous. There simply were not enough Indians left to fight off the increasing influx of white settlers.

In 1824, the U.S. Government created the Bureau of Indian Affairs, housed, notably, within the War Department. In 1830, led by President Andrew Jackson (1767–1845), a staunch advocate of Native American removal to western lands, the U.S. Government passed the Indian Removal Bill. This gave Jackson the authority to "transfer any eastern tribe to trans-Mississippi areas [west of the Mississippi River]." Creeks, Cherokee, and some Seminoles were among the most deeply affected, being forcibly evicted from their ancestral lands. Continuing the conversion efforts of the first colonists, missionaries from the major Protestant denominations often either joined these migrations or established schools and churches when the tribes reached their new homes.

Reservations: Removed from Home

Given a growing American emphasis on good Christian behavior in the 19th century, extermination of Native peoples became more and more difficult to justify and the popularity of policies to entirely eliminate Native peoples waned. Where tribes were not destroyed through genocide (the destruction of an entire people or ethnic group), more "civilized" approaches were taken by the federal government in which tribes were simply removed from their homelands to areas of the country for which whites had no use, or to reservations created by treaties to keep Indians away from white interests.

An example of one such removal in the 1830s became known as the Trail of Tears (see page 37). Tribes such as the Cherokee and Chickasaw were forcibly removed to Oklahoma, then part of Indian Territory. This practice not only settled disputes over land and natural resources, but also further disrupted the cultures of the tribes whose traditions, values, and beliefs were so closely linked to their homelands.

Unfortunately, greed for land would soon result in white encroachment upon Indian Territory. This came as intertribal conflicts resulting from the removal were already plaguing many Native groups.

"OURS"

Throughout United States history, there have been deliberate attempts by mainstream American institutions such as government agencies, schools, and churches, to destroy the Native American institutions of family, clan, and tribal structure, religious belief systems and practices, customs, and traditional way of life. The Dakota writer Vine Deloria, Jr. in his 1988 book *Custer Died for Your Sins*, wrote, "When questioned by an anthropologist on what the Indians called America before the white man came, an Indian said simply, 'Ours.'"

As Native American nations west of the Mississippi were defeated militarily, they were forced to relinquish vast portions of their homeland and offered in return small portions of land known as reservations, to which they had to relocate. These reservations were often lands that whites did not want because they were harsh environments that offered little in the way of resources and opportunity for survival.

Forced to Change Their Ways

As "defeated nations," Native American tribes were expected to surrender their so-called "savage ways" and be absorbed and assimilated into white society. The federal government wanted to "civilize" the

The Trail of Tears

The Cherokee Nation was one of the strongest and largest tribes in America in the early 1800s. Some of its members had traveled to Europe, the teacher Sequoyah (1776–1843) had developed the first written language for the Cherokee in 1821. The tribe even had a newspaper.

However, in 1838, after resisting for years with military and political maneuvers, the Cherokee people were nearly all captured and placed in camps by the U.S. Army. After lengthy negotiations, the Cherokee finally agreed, reluctantly, to leave their home in North Carolina and Arkansas and relocate to the West. On October 1, 1838, already weakened and sick from being forced into the camps, the people set out on foot on their 1,200-mile journey.

It was a grueling trip and thousands of Cherokee died along the way. More than four months later, they arrived at the land inside Indian Territory that had been established as their new home (in what is today Oklahoma). Their long march became a low point in the history of Native American relations, and is known today as The Trail of Tears.

Native Americans, and the churches wanted to "Christianize" them. Thus, the popular saying of this period from about 1860 to the 1930s was, "Kill the Indian, but save the man."

Sitting Bull (see page 101), the Lakota Chief, said of this policy of assimilation (quoted in Vine Deloria's 1994 book *God Is Red: A Native View of Religion*), "I am a red man. If the Great Spirit had desired me to be a white man, he would have made me so in the first place. He put in your heart certain wishes and plans, in my heart he put other and different desires. Each man is good in His sight. It is not necessary for eagles to be crows."

As it became increasingly apparent that Native Americans had no interest in adopting white cultural standards and practices, whites turned to the power of education to "civilize" Native American children early in life. Most treaty agreements included provisions for the education of Native American youth by establishing church-affiliated schools. Native American children were deliberately taken from their homes at a young age and forced to attend boarding schools as far away from home as possible. In the government-supported, church-run boarding schools, whose purpose was to assimilate Native Americans, the children were not allowed to speak their native language or practice their cultural traditions (this was often enforced through harsh physical punishment). They were required to speak only English, practice Christianity, and learn the rules of white society. Moreover, these children, who had been removed from their homes typically around age four or five, usually spent a minimum of eight years away from their families and communities, with no visits home.

Upon returning to their communities, many of these individuals discovered very quickly that they were not culturally "white," yet they were not "Indian" either. What resulted was an intergenerational division that today remains a powerful influence on the cultural identity of many Native Americans—particularly older generations, who still show the effects of this childhood trauma and carry a great deal of shame about who they are.

Conclusion: Clash and Blend

With the coming of the Europeans, things changed rapidly for Native American people. The colonists and explorers came from Europe with new ideas, new religions, new technology, new diseases. Just how many Native people lived in North America when the Europeans arrived is unknown. Estimates range from a few million to tens of millions. What is certain is that the Native American population fell dramatically when the strangers from Europe arrived, plummeting to perhaps fewer than a million people by the end of the 19th century.

Most American history books have ignored or marginalized the history of the Native American tribes. But the first Europeans to arrive in the Americas would not have survived without the assistance of the Native peoples (see chapter 3). The majority of the new immigrants who came to this country came out of the cities of Britain, France, Germany, and other western European countries. They had no knowledge of the natural world, how to plant, cultivate, and harvest the crops the Native peoples used. The Native Americans gave them food, land, and new ways of living. In return, Native people gained access to new technology, new religions, and new ways of living. It was a mutual exchange, at first, between two equals.

As immigration to the New World increased, the Native peoples were exposed to new diseases, new vices, and violence. Great epidemics of smallpox, cholera, and other communicable diseases decimated entire towns or tribes of Native Americans. Alcohol, virtually unknown until the Europeans came, not only killed because of its use, but devastated Native communities because of its misuse. Firearms and gunpowder, also unknown among Native American nations, was introduced as a weapon of the Europeans and given to the Native people, which they used against one another. While some tribes were almost constantly battling their neighbors, war, on a scale that Europeans knew very well, was something the Native American had not encountered before.

Amid such destruction came new religious ideas. The Native people picked up the myriad versions of Christianity practiced by the Europeans and shaped it to fit their own views of the world. The story of the continuing blending—and clashing—of these two worlds will be the story of Native Americans in the chapters that follow.

Key Events in Native American History

THE STORY OF NATIVE AMERICANS IN A LAND RAPIDLY BEING overtaken by settlers from Europe is a series of conflicts. There is not room here to include every event that had an impact, since, as we have already mentioned in the introduction, Native Americans comprise many tribes, rather than a single people. Each tribe has its own story of the struggle to survive in the new world created by the arrival of Europeans. However, we have chosen key events that have the widest resonance or where the faith and spirituality of Native Americans played a significant role. This chapter focuses on events that occurred in the 19th and 20th centuries.

Note that there are several examples of Native Americans who had visions or dreams, and then spread the messages they received in those dreams to their people. The belief in the power of dreams and visions is strong in Native American tradition, and these visionaries were taken very seriously.

Handsome Lake's Visions

Native Americans place great faith in visions experienced by people they think of as prophets. One prophet whose visions had a long-lasting impact was Handsome Lake (1735–1815), a Seneca prophet who lived in upstate New York. The Seneca were part of the Iroquois Confederacy, a gathering of six tribes in the region. During the years of the American Revolution and just after, the tribes suffered greatly from disease, political infighting, and the growing presence of American settlers on their lands. They were also faced with the continuing efforts of Americans to bring Christianity to their lives.

Amid this, Handsome Lake, whose name in his native language was Skaniadariio, experienced his first vision after drinking heavily following the death of his daughter in 1799. In the vision he was taken on a journey to the afterlife, where he met Jesus Christ and other figures, and saw visions of what life was like after death. His response to these visions was to begin preaching a new way of life for his people.

He had more visions that further expanded his knowledge, and he created what amounted to a gospel, the Gaiwiio, that described how his people should live. Handsome Lake preached that people should repent (or confess) their various sins. He also spoke against the use of alcohol, against abortions, and for the regular use of sacred ceremonies such as the Thanksgiving Dance and the Feather Dance. His visions seemed to combine traditional Native American beliefs with some of the influences of Christianity.

His new religion spread to all the six tribes of the Iroquois Confederacy, but after his death, his influence faded. In the 1840s, his grandson Sosheowa, also known as Jimmy Johnson, brought Handsome Lake's teachings back and created the Code of Handsome Lake. The religion based on that code is still practiced on Iroquois reservations. At every other annual Six Nations meeting, the code is recited by preachers.

Manifest Destiny

As seen in chapter 1, the establishment of Indian Territory in 1830 created a legal framework for the forced resettlement of Native Americans. A philosophy known as Manifest Destiny gave the continuing removal efforts a philosophical justification.

In 1845, a newspaper editor named John O'Sullivan wrote an editorial in *United States Magazine and Democratic Review* that said America had been given "a manifest destiny to overspread and to possess the whole of the continent which Providence has given us for the development of the great experiment of liberty." By "manifest," he meant "obvious," and he gave a name to an idea that had long been a part of the American mind: That God had granted the European settlers of this

PRECEDING PAGE
Forced to leave home
Over several decades in the late 1800s, the federal government forced Native Americans to relocate away from their ancestral homes to new and distant lands. This 1966 painting by Valjean McCarty Hessing, is called Choctaw Removal *and depicts one of those relocations.*

new land the right and duty to essentially conquer all the continent, regardless of who lived there to begin with.

Manifest Destiny became the underpinning for much of the legislation that followed—laws that, step by step, removed more and more Native Americans from their land. And land, for the Native Americans, is significant in every part of their physical and spiritual lives. Uprooting Native Americans in this fashion can be compared to uprooting a tree. Without the earth, the land, the tree cannot grow. Plant it in an unfamiliar ground and it will not grow, either. Manifest Destiny, to many, justified this vast uprooting.

In 1846, James K. Polk (1795–1849) was elected president largely on the strength of his fervent support for Manifest Destiny. Under Polk, removal of Native peoples continued unabated and battles with Native Americans occurred in many areas of the country. The Americans rallied under the banner of Manifest Destiny, sure that they were sent by God to do this work. This not only meant that they should possess the land, but also that they needed to bring Christianity to the Native Americans.

Incidents Out West

In the years before the Civil War (1861–1865), a variety of treaties and agreements with Native Americans were ignored as settlers spread out across the West. In California, a Spanish plan to have the mission priests hold land until the Native Americans could be "trained well enough" to take it back was scuttled when the 1849 Gold Rush swelled California with new settlers.

Apache and Navajo tribes were slowly pushed out of the New Mexico territory, also to make room for settlers and miners. In Illinois and later Kansas, the Kickapoo chief and medicine man Kenekuk (c.1790–1852) instructed his followers not to learn English, not to sign away their land, and to maintain their traditional customs.

One of the most grievous incidents occurred in northern California in 1860. As described in Paula Mitchell Marks's 1998 book *In a Barren Land*, a group of Native Americans from the Wiyot tribe tried to return to a sacred place local settlers called Indian Island. It was believed by the tribe to be the center of the world and was the place where all their ceremonies were held. Marks quotes historian Jack Norton, "The ceremony they had come to perform was comparable to the high mass [in Catholicism]. If you believe that you are responsible for

SMOHALLA AND THE DREAMERS

Like Tenskwatawa (page 100), the prophet Smohalla (1815?–1907) was believed to have died but then came back to his people, the Wanapan, with a powerful story to tell. Smohalla was killed in a battle, but several years later he returned and said that he had been taken to the Spirit World beyond death, where he learned that the day was coming in which the white people would leave the land. The movement these visions inspired was called the Dreamers or the Washani, and it spread throughout the Northwest, home of the Wanapan.

The religion also spread to the Nez Perce tribe. Influenced by Smohalla's teachings, the great Nez Perce leader Chief Joseph (c.1840–1904) led a series of battles against encroaching American settlers. Chief Joseph attracted much attention and was regarded as a great warrior, but he was eventually defeated. The end of his campaign also effectively ended the spread of the Dreamers religion.

keeping the world in balance, you have a duty to do it no matter what. They must have looked around them and seen the collapse of everything they knew. The most natural thing for them to do was go to the center, go to God."

Showing an intense disrespect, in some cases hatred, for Native traditions that characterized American actions throughout the West, settlers from nearby Eureka met the Wiyots on the island and murdered them all.

The Long Walk

In 1863, Bureau of Indian Affairs officials sought to move the Navajos of the Southwest onto a reservation at Bosque Redondo in New Mexico. Tied by long-held beliefs in the sacred nature of their land, the tribe did not want to leave. Their chief, Barboncito (1820–1871), as quoted in Russell's book, said there was a deep connection between land and spirit. "When the Navajos were first created four mountains and four rivers were pointed out to us, inside of which we should live. That was to be our country and was given to us by the first woman of the Navajo tribe. It was told to us by our forefathers that we were never to move east of the Rio Grande or west of the San Juan Rivers."

But the federal government gave the Navajos an ultimatum, saying that after July 20, 1863, any Navajo found within that land would be treated as hostile and captured or killed. Not long afterward, American troops poured into the region, killing Navajos, chasing away livestock, and destroying crops. Finally, beginning in early 1864, the Navajos began, reluctantly, to leave their ancestral land, making what would become known as The Long Walk more than 250 miles to their new home. Although what was left of the tribe was allowed to return to their land in 1868, the event was a striking example of the attitude of American government officials to the deeply-held beliefs of Native Americans.

Indian Wars

Inspired partly by their spiritual connections to the land, but also by their absolute opposition to the continuing efforts of Americans to remove them, several Native American leaders in the years after the Civil War led bloody revolts against their treatment. The most well-known of these so-called Indian Wars was with the Sioux in the Black Hills of South Dakota.

This 19th-century illustration depicts life in early California. The role of the Catholic missionaries has become a much debated one. While they were bringing their faith to the Native population, they also brought disease and other troubles.

An 1871 act of Congress removed the official "nation" status of Native American tribes; before that, there was an understanding that dealing with a tribe was like dealing with a sovereign (independent) nation. After the act was passed, treaties were revamped to allow more access to what had been Native American reservations and land. The Sioux vehemently resisted all offers to buy their land or attempts to drive them off it. In January 1876, the government ordered all Sioux to either report to one of six reservations or be forcibly removed to those areas by the U.S. Army.

The Sioux chief Crazy Horse (see page 103) led his forces against U.S. Army troops in several successful engagements. The most famous battle occurred at the Little Bighorn River on June 25, 1876. Sioux and Cheyenne warriors overwhelmed Seventh Cavalry forces led by General George Armstrong Custer (1939–1876), killing all 265 soldiers. The warriors had been inspired to battle by a vision experienced by Sitting Bull (see page 101) another Sioux chief, in which "he saw soldiers riding upside through the sky toward an Indian village," Marks wrote.

Other violent clashes occurred in these years between U.S. soldiers and the Nez Perce in the Northwest; Cheyenne leader Dull Knife

(1810–1883) in the Dakota territories; and the Apaches of Arizona, led by Geronimo (1829–1909).

The Spirit Dance and the Massacre at Wounded Knee

As the Indian Wars on the Great Plains were coming to an end with disastrous defeats of the Native Americans, who were almost always badly outnumbered, another visionary started a movement that had a sad and violent end but whose impact resonated for another century. The father of the Paiute man Wovoka (1856–1932) had been a respected prophet and visionary; he experienced vivid dreams that he and his people believed foretold the future. When Wovoka himself experienced visions and dreams, people paid close attention. As a young man in Nevada, his dreams led him to create the Spirit Dance, or Ghost Dance, a ceremony in which dancers communicated with the spirits of their ancestors. The goal of the dancing was also to liberate the people from the invasion of white settlers.

On January 1, 1889, while Wovoka was in the midst of a high fever and experiencing new visions, there was a total eclipse of the sun. This enhanced his reputation and helped solidify the power of his teachings. Wovoka said he had taken a spiritual journey to visit the Creator, and that he had been told his people should live in peace. The Spirit Dance movement spread quickly, and tribes from many areas sent people to Wovoka to learn about his visions. The Spirit Dance itself was soon seen in many places around the West.

At the time, the United States government was continuing to remove Native Americans from their lands in often-violent conflicts. The Spirit Dance was seen as a revolutionary movement—a focus for Native Americans to resist these resettlement plans. Spirit Dancers were attacked on several occasions, but the most deadly attack came on December 29, 1890, when U.S. Army troops opened fire on Native Americans at Wounded Knee in South Dakota.

Although Wovoka denied he ever said it, there was a rumor among Spirit Dancers that the shirts they wore were bulletproof. This proved fatally incorrect. The massacre not only killed more than 150 people, but also helped bring the movement almost to an end. However, as we will see later in this chapter (page 50), the location of the Wounded Knee massacre would once again become a touchstone for the ongoing clashes between Native American and European American cultures.

Peyote Religion

The use of peyote, a type of cactus bud that produces psychedelic or hallucinogenic effects when eaten, is an ancient practice among cultures in the Americas. In the late 19th century, several Southwestern Native American tribes began to use peyote in more organized religious contexts. In peyote religions, followers eat small portions of peyote, called *buttons*, sing songs, and perform a variety of ceremonies. In many cases, they blend Christian beliefs and ideas with the traditional use of peyote, which they say gives them a higher and deeper understanding of and connection to the spiritual world.

As the practice spread more formally, opposition arose on local and federal levels and a variety of legislation was passed banning the practice. (Some tribes, such as the Navajo in 1940, also later tried to outlaw the use of peyote.) The objections came about because of peyote's drug-like nature. Just as people objected to alcohol or marijuana use, they felt that peyote was a narcotic. Some users were jailed, and raids were carried out on ceremonies while they were under way.

Followers kept using the substance, however, and in 1918 in Oklahoma, they formed the Native American Church as a way to help protect their practices. Similar groups were founded in other states, and in 1944 a national Native American Church group was founded. In defending itself against the legal challenges it faced, the Church argued that its use of peyote is a sacrament of their church, similar to the Christian Eucharist. (The Eucharist is the ceremony in which Christians remember Christ's Last Supper; they eat bread and wine that has been consecrated according to their denomination's beliefs.)

Although it has never had a widespread following, the peyote religions remain a part of Native American religious practices in some places. One problem the group faced was an influx of non-Native Americans who wanted to join to experience peyote's effects for non-spiritual reasons. By the 1980s, the group had withdrawn from most contact with non-Native Americans.

In 1994, President Bill Clinton signed an amendment to 1978 American Indian Religious Freedom Act, which had been passed to help Native Americans practice their traditional faiths free of restrictions. The 1994 amendment, among other things, legalized the use of peyote in religious ceremonies (even by members of U.S. military forces). Today, peyote religions are practiced in some form by perhaps 25 percent of Native Americans, according to the book *A Native American Theology*, written in 2002 by Clara Sue Kidwell and others. The

Black Elk Speaks

The Lakota holy man Black Elk (1863–1950) was perhaps the most influential spiritual guide in the past 100 years that the wider world has had to the life of Native Americans. Black Elk experienced several visions as a young man, and, as a result,. he became a medicine man, or spiritual leader, in 1881. He traveled widely in the West, living in Wyoming, Montana, and also traveling with Buffalo Bill's Wild West Show. In 1890, he was present at the massacre at Wounded Knee.

In 1904, he was baptized as a Catholic, however, and began a long career of teaching the Catholic faith to others.

His knowledge of traditional Native American ways and his experiences as a medicine man were shared with the wider world in 1932 with the publication of *Black Elk Speaks*. A Nebraska poet named John Neihardt (1881–1973) interviewed Black Elk several times and wrote down his remembrances. This in-depth look at Native American spirituality, religious practices, and interpretation of Christianity remains a classic work in Native American studies.

In recent years, some critics have debated the accuracy of some of Neihardt's work. But the book, and several others Black Elk wrote with Neihardt and other scholars, remains an insightful look at Native American spiritual life.

authors describe peyote use in churches that are both Christian and more traditionally Native American.

Alcatraz

In 1952, the U.S. government once again adopted a policy to relocate Native Americans. Large numbers of them were moved from various reservations in the West into relocation centers near major California cities. The basic idea behind the policy was to eliminate tribal distinctions and "give" the tribes independence. In reality, the effect of such a policy was to further weaken and ultimately destroy any sense of tribal identity among Native Americans.

This policy was not well received, and it helped encourage a nascent movement among Native Americans, mostly younger people, to resist in some way. The policy continued during the 1960s—a decade which also saw widespread social change such as the Civil Rights Movement among African Americans.

A number of Indian activists saw a chance to make a statement about the importance of civil rights for Native Americans and to call attention to the ongoing relocation program. In 1969 they organized the takeover of Alcatraz Island in San Francisco Bay in California. On the island was a prison that had once been the most notorious in the nation. The prison had closed in 1963 and was empty when the activists arrived to claim it.

They quickly caught the nation's attention, earning support from activists in other causes and from celebrities such as Jane Fonda and Marlon Brando. The group remained on the island for more than 18 months. Many lived there full-time, while others came and went. Some of the Alcatraz activists were also active in the American Indian Movement (AIM) in 1968 (see page 83), which had become the driving force behind the ongoing Native American rights movement.

The administration of President Richard M. Nixon negotiated with the activists, and eventually the group left the island peacefully. Not long after, the controversial relocation program was ended.

The Alcatraz takeover remains a key moment in the modern struggle for Native American rights. In 1999, a 30th anniversary celebration was held on the island. "Alcatraz made it OK to be a native person," California State University at San Francisco teacher Lee Davis told the *San Francisco Chronicle* on October 24, 1999. "People came out

Comforts of home

Protesters who took over Alcatraz Island in 1969 had time to relax and play basketball while occupying the former prison in an effort to raise consciousness about treatment of Native Americans.

of the woodwork to claim their identity. It revived languages and cultural history. The consequences of Alcatraz were quite remarkable."

Return to Wounded Knee

The work of AIM continued after Alcatraz. On February 23, 1973, the group led representatives of more than 75 tribes back to Wounded Knee in South Dakota and "reclaimed" the area for the Lakota nation. The site of the 1890 massacre became a rallying point for Native Americans around the nation. The activists demanded a reorganization of the Bureau of Indian Affairs, which they called corrupt and inept. They demanded an investigation by the Senate into misuse of tribal funds by the U.S. government, and they objected to strip mining on the site of Wounded Knee and in surrounding areas.

The federal government moved quickly to try to remove the activists from the site, surrounding it with marshals and federal troops. The takeover quickly became a siege, as government forces tried to cut off supplies to the Native Americans camped there. Within the camp, the people tried to live in as many traditional ways as possible. Marriages were celebrated, birth ceremonies were held, and other spiritual ceremonies were completed.

The siege went on for 71 days, through cold weather, even though bursts of fighting killed two of the activists and two FBI agents. Eventually, they surrendered; more than 1,200 people were arrested. The event became a touchstone in the struggle between Native Americans and the United States government.

Gambling Comes to Reservations

Although it did not directly affect Native American faith or spirituality, the passage of a federal act allowing gambling on Native American land was the most significant event of the past 25 years for the Native community. The Indian Gaming Regulatory Act of 1988 first allowed "traditional Indian low-stakes gambling done as part of ceremonies," but it also let tribes work out agreements with state governments for additional gaming. Within only six years, the nationwide Native American gambling industry was generating more than $6 billion in annual revenue, mostly tax-free. In 2001, the nearly 300 Native casinos earned more than $12 billion in revenue.

Native American tribes have been legally able to build these casinos because they own the land they live on. The sovereignty they hold over the land has been established by treaties over the years. This, as we saw earlier, was rooted in their spiritual connection to the land and the integral part specific pieces of land play in their belief systems.

The impact of all this money on the tribes that built the casinos has been enormous. New buildings have been built, new programs for tribal members have been created, and new land has been bought and annexed to enlarge the reservation. The political power of the tribes has increased dramatically, too, as their new-found wealth enables them to contribute to politicians' campaigns and lobby local governments, often successfully.

Although the huge increase in reservation casinos has been controversial in some places—some people argue that this is just another example of white people taking advantage of Native Americans and that many of the profits are not going to the tribes themselves—the growth continues. (This issue will be covered in detail in chapter 5.)

STRIP MINING

Working a mine from the earth's surface by stripping away the land above and around the substance being mined. Strip mining destroys the surrounding environment.

3

From Moccasins to Music: Cultural Influences

THERE IS A LAKOTA ELDER WHO OCCASIONALLY INTRODUCES HIMSELF by saying, "Hello, my name is Joe, welcome to my country." Native American humor can be subtle, but at times also quite direct. Joe's greeting lends an important perspective to the history of the Americas. Indeed, Native Americans were the first groups of people to "discover America," and have in many ways made it what it is today.

The perspective of history is often focused on how Europeans have used Native American contributions to culture, rather than on what those contributions were. As noted earlier, what became the United States was an evolved, diverse, and complex set of individual societies long before the Europeans arrived. Individually and collectively, these tribes have left legacies behind in nearly every aspect of life today. Consider these few of the many Native American contributions to what has become the United States.

Agriculture and Food

Europeans who arrived in the eastern part of what would become the United States were woefully unprepared for life in their new land. They brought with them only the traditional European practices of finding or growing food, techniques that were perfect for European weather and environment, but often inadequate for North America. Perhaps the first and most important contribution made by the Native peoples these colonists encountered was learning how to survive.

Native Americans taught early colonial settlers new ways to hunt and fish. For example, Native people caught their fish in nets called weirs that were made from reeds woven or tied together. They placed the weir across a stream and anchored it with rocks or poles stuck into the sand. The European ways of fishing with large nets did not work well in smaller American streams and rivers.

In addition, Native Americans hunted big animals such as deer, bear, and buffalo, mostly with bows and arrows. Europeans had to learn from Native Americans how to stalk local game. The colonists brought with them guns—loud and inefficient muskets that did not work in bad weather. The Native methods and technology made it possible to hunt at all times.

It is interesting to note a longstanding tradition among many Native Americans regarding hunting: Before or right after killing an animal for food, the hunter gives thanks to the animal for providing its life so that the hunter and his family might live. This goes directly to the continuing, deep connection between Native Americans and the natural world.

Again in the colonial days, Native American cooking techniques were more effective than the traditional European methods colonists brought with them. Often, Native people cooked their fish and meat over a grill made of reeds or sticks. However, most of the cooking was done in clay pots that were placed on the fire to boil. In this way, they would cook vegetables, fruits, nuts, roots, and meat together. Learning to adapt to the local products meant the colonists had to learn Native recipes for cooking these foods.

Native Americans also planted gardens much like today's kitchen gardens. They grew beans, peas, melons, pumpkins, sunflowers, potatoes, and many other foods, and shared these crops and information about how to grow them with to newly-arrived European settlers.

That early history reflects the continuing contribution of Native knowledge to the field of agriculture. When we go to the movies and eat popcorn, we are eating a product created by Native Americans. When we have guacamole, which is made from avocados, we can thank early Native farmers who first harvested this fruit.

The list of other foods first domesticated (grown for cultivation) by Native Americans is a long one and includes more than 40 plants, including corn (or maize), white potato, pumpkins, squash, red peppers, peanuts, popcorn, peas, green beans, tomatoes, strawberries, and tobacco. Of the leading food crops grown all over the world, approximately 42 percent by weight is composed of three Native American crops: corn, potatoes, and peanuts. Measured in dollar value, approximately 48 percent of the leading food and economic crops produced in the United States were first domesticated by Native Americans. We can also thank the Maya from what is today Central America for a very popular food from plants: chocolate.

Beyond food crops, plants first domesticated by Native Americans include indigo, an important clothing dye; gourds, which were used as canteens and as containers of various sorts; cotton, one of the world's most important crops for making clothing; and decorative flowers such as marigolds, dahlias, and zinnias.

It is perhaps appropriate that this long-lasting and literally life-giving set of contributions to world culture is from the land, which has such deep spiritual connection for all Native Americans.

Thanksgiving: More than Just Turkey

Thanksgiving is an American holiday that is believed to have originated from initial celebrations between European colonists (such as the Pilgrims in Massachusetts) and Native Americans of social harmony and abundance at the time of harvest. However, Giving Thanks is an age-old Native American tradition that extends well beyond the celebration of a once-a-year holiday. The tradition of Giving Thanks is, and always has been, an ongoing part of Native culture. In the early colonial days, that tradition was combined with a European harvest celebration to create the Thanksgiving holiday that is celebrated today.

For Native Americans, Giving Thanks is a way of life in which harmony and balance with one's universe are essential. They are keenly aware of the importance of maintaining proper relations with the spirits of guides, ancestors, and the natural surroundings, because many of these spirits are considered the source of the bounty of the earth. Native traditionalists offer thanks to the spirits with the hope that they will be generous in the coming hunting or planting season, among other ongoing activities that affect tribal communities.

Historically, it is unclear exactly when the first Thanksgiving celebration took place. However, the event probably most closely associated with today's national holiday was a harvest celebration that occurred between the Puritans at Plymouth Plantation, Massachusetts, and the surrounding Native people. After arriving the previous fall and surviving a harrowing winter with the help of a Native American man named Squanto, the Puritan settlers at Plymouth Plantation held their first Thanksgiving feast in the fall of 1621.

To celebrate the harvest, continuing an autumn European tradition, they invited their neighbors, who included Wampanoag Chief Massasoit (1585–1656) and about 90 of his men. Among the bounties they enjoyed at this celebration were fowl (which included turkey, quail, ducks, and geese), venison (which the Native people provided), and probably fish and shellfish. Boiled pumpkin, corn cakes, and pudding were also enjoyed. These may have been supplemented with wild nuts and berries, as well as the popcorn that was provided by Massasoit's brother, Quadequina.

Although the holiday was sporadically celebrated from the time of the Revolution, it was not until 1863 that it was proclaimed a national day of Thanksgiving by President Abraham Lincoln. Initially Thanksgiving day was set for August 6, but Sara Josepha Hale (1788–1879), editor of *Godey's Lady's Book*, and Secretary of State William Seward (1801–1872) persuaded Lincoln to change the date to encompass the harvest festival traditions of many New England states. In 1941, President Franklin Roosevelt made the fourth Thursday in November a federal holiday for Thanksgiving.

Throughout the course of these historical events, Native Americans in different parts of the country continued Giving Thanks at various times throughout the year as a part of their ceremonial traditions, many of which have survived and continue to flourish.

Sports and Games

Competition has always been very important and even sacred to the Native American tribes, and is a part of their traditional way of life. Sport and games had many purposes in early, traditional Native life, including serving as a form of ceremony, settling disputes, teaching the skills necessary for survival, and symbolizing processes and cycles that occur in nature.

The games in earlier years included bow and arrow, blowgun (where a dart is blown through a hollow tube), and Indian ball. The games were for ceremonial purposes and special events, such as Fall Festival, or for competition among tribal clans.

The Native American culture places much ceremony on pre-game activities using plants, water, and prayer-chants. In most tribal traditions, it is important to take part in a special ceremony with a Medicine Man or Woman before and after the competition to give participants strength and clarity. The Cherokee, for example, used a ceremony called Deer Rider to ask the spirits to guide them during competition. In addition, it is important to realize that Native American sports and games often focused more on group competitions than on individual competitions and honor was often more important than winning.

Besides Jim Thorpe (see the box on page 60), there were other Native Americans who achieved fame in professional sports, such as Charles "Chief" Bender (1884–1954) of the Chippewa tribe, a pitcher for the Philadelphia Athletics from 1903 to 1917. Bender pitched in five World Series and was elected to the Baseball Hall of Fame in 1953.

The sport of running produced several Native American champions. Tom Longboat (1887–1947) of the Onondaga tribe in New York

Influence on Clothing

Different Native tribes wore different clothing and other adornments, depending on the time period. Early on, many Native people wore clothes made from deer skins or buffalo hide, among other animals. Earrings, necklaces, and bracelets were worn by men and women. This jewelry was made from bone, copper, shell, and polished stone beads. Most men wore their hair long. Women usually had long hair with bangs across the forehead.

Both men and women wore braid wraps that were decorated with certain beads. The types of beads they chose was one way to show which tribe they belonged to. Of course, both clothing and other adornments varied from tribe to tribe.

Among some of the other contributions of Native American clothing to today's Americans are moccasins and ponchos. In addition, the chaps that rodeo riders wear today over their pants are a form of Native leather leggings.

Native jewelry is seen in many places today, worn by women of all backgrounds. Native people also were among the first to harvest and use cotton, which is used today to make much of the clothing we wear.

won the Boston Marathon in 1907 with a record time. Ellison Brown of the Narragansett tribe in Rhode Island won the Boston Marathon in 1936 and again in 1939, also setting new records. Billy Mills (b.1938), an Oglala Lakota, earned worldwide fame in the 1964 Olympics. The unheralded Mills stunned the world with a come-from-behind victory in the 10,000-meter race, setting a new world record and winning the first Olympic gold medal for a Native American

The annual Eskimo Olympics feature traditional competitions among Aleut and Inuit Native people. The sports in these games are based on ancient skills needed for hunting and for survival in the harsh Northern lands. At the Eskimo Olympics, athletes compete in the knuckle-hop, the ear-pull (a sort of tug-of-war with ears), the four-man carry, and the sealskin toss (a kind of human-powered trampoline).

Music, Dance, and Ceremony

Music for Native Americans starts with the drum, either hand-held or large powwow drums (one large drum beat by several drummers simultaneously). Drumming is considered the heartbeat of Mother Earth.

Vocal sounds are combined with chants and the rattle and drums to form the basis of Native American music. Rocks in baskets, seeds in gourds, whistles, and reed flutes can also be used. The songs are usually in the tribal languages, with syllables used in harmonic rhythm, such as the Cherokee Corn Dance Song, "*Ho we ye lo ye, Ye go wa lu ye, Ho we lo ye.*" The sounds mimic planting work in the corn fields, much as the sounds of work are used in other cultural songs. Steady beats are common in the music, with a lead singer starting the song and others following with voice and instruments.

Dances are usually in circle patterns with lead male and female dancers. The dances are most often introduced with stories of animals in nature, children playing, putting children to sleep, playing games, and sharing stories of memorable events.

With traditional songs and modern instrumentation, such as a variety of flutes and amplification, there is a renewal of interest among young people that has brought these wonderful old sounds to many other listeners to enjoy. In many places, annual powwow gatherings are open to the public, who can come and watch these traditional, celebratory, and sacred dances. There are even competitions among dance groups that are judged by tribal leaders.

Tools of his trade
This collection of memorabilia from Native American athlete Jim Thorpe points out not only his versatility—he starred at football and baseball, among other sports—but also his heritage. He made the traditional beaded gloves, at bottom left, himself while at the Carlisle (Pennsylvania) Indian school.

Traditional ceremonies are also being revived by many tribes. Among these are the Green Corn and Eagle dances, the Sun Dance, the Spirit Dance, and many other ceremonial traditions. These ceremonies provide an opportunity to renew the traditional ceremonial and sacred ways of the past for the Native Americans of the future.

The Indian Self-Determination and Education Assistance Act of 1975 and the American Indian Religious Freedom Act (AIRFA) in 1978 recognized the right of worship on Indian reservations. A wide variety of cultural development projects and programs by the tribes have done much to revive the traditions, languages, and ceremonies that make Native American people unique.

In addition, non-Native Americans have in recent decades taken a greater interest in the music and dance of indigenous people. The "world music" revival has included Native American music along with the sounds created by people around the world. Groups such as Emmy-nominated Blackfire, comprised of Navajo brothers; Mary Youngblood, a singer-songwriter; and R. Carlos Nakai, a Navajo-Ute who is the world's

"The Greatest Athlete in the World"

Jim Thorpe (1887–1953), a Sac/Fox/Potawatomi, is one of the most famous and versatile athletes in history, of any ancestry.

While at Carlisle Indian School in Pennsylvania from 1904 to 1912, he earned varsity letters in 11 sports: football, baseball, track, boxing, wrestling, lacrosse, gymnastics, swimming, hockey, handball, and basketball.

He led Carlisle to unprecedented heights in football, defeating the best all-white Eastern champions and winning the national championship in 1912.

Thorpe earned his greatest fame at the 1912 Olympic Games in Stockholm, Sweden. There he became the only athlete ever to win both the decathlon (combining 10 track and field events) and pentathlon (five events).

By all accounts, Thorpe was a modest man, well-grounded in the Native tradition that people share their status no matter what they have achieved. In preparation for the medal ceremony following his victory in the decathlon, Thorpe was told it is the custom to kneel in the presence of the Swedish king. When the King of Sweden congratulated him by saying, "Sir, you are the greatest athlete in the world," Thorpe remained standing and reportedly replied, "Thanks, King."

Unfortunately, both of Thorpe's medals were taken from him by the Amateur Athletic Union (AAU) due to a controversy over whether he had accepted money to play minor league baseball prior to the Games. At the time, professionals of any sport were barred from Olympic competition.

The overly harsh ruling struck Thorpe from the record books. It was not until 1982 that his supporters succeeded in having Thorpe's Olympic gold medals and this records reinstated.

After the Olympics, Thorpe played professional football and baseball and went on to coach college and professional teams. In 1950 the Associated Press voted him the Greatest Athlete of the Half-Century. He died in 1953 at the age of 64.

premier Native flutist, have helped popularize Native American music. In addition, more well-known artists such as Neil Young, Jackson Browne, and Los Lobos have incorporated some Native musicians or themes into their songs.

Literature

Since the beginning of time, Native peoples have used a strong oral tradition of storytelling to preserve and strengthen their cultures by ensuring that each passing generation carries forward the wisdom and ways of the previous ones. Stories, songs, and chants were interwoven with all aspects of life, including healing ceremonies, planting crops, hunting, welcoming family and friends, and so on.

The stories were considered to carry a great deal of power by offering a valuable lesson or message, or as a way of simply connecting with others. In particular, elders were responsible for teaching children the values, beliefs, and customs of the family, clan, and tribe through stories that showed children not only how to think and act, but also how to listen. Stories explained everything from how the world was made, to how the first people originated, to how the specific place, plant, or animal that was sacred to that tribe came to be, to how people should treat one another.

By the end of the 1700s, mostly non-Native people were attempting to put the Native oral traditions into written form. By the late 1800s, anthropologists were seeking assistance from Native storytellers to create a formal record of ritual narratives, chants, songs, prayers, and sayings, stories, tales, and formulas. Not long after, Native people began writing down their own stories. The Cherokee leader Sequoyah (1776–1843) is famous for helping develop the first known written alphabet for a Native language in 1821. Today, the process of preserving a variety of languages now spoken by only a few elderly tribal members is ongoing. Interest has increased among younger Native Americans to learn and help preserve these ancient tongues.

Although the use of writing and alphabets spread quickly among Native tribes, before the 1960s there was little interest in Native

Drum circle
The tradition of group drumming remains a part of modern Native American ceremonies and music, as it has been for centuries.

American literature. That began to change in 1969 when N. Scott Momaday (b.1934), a Kiowa writer, won the Pulitzer Prize for his novel *House Made of Dawn*. Today, many Native American writers draw upon the age-old customs and wisdom of this oral tradition of storytelling to tell both historical and contemporary stories of Native American life. Their experiences and their particular world view has exposed the whole world to Native American culture and has helped call attention to the ongoing plight of many members of the Native American community. In addition, their work helps to continue and preserve the long-standing traditions of their tribes.

The Relationship to the World

One of the greatest Native American contributions to today's America is a view of the world and a way of life that emphasizes the idea that everything is alive and that nothing should be wasted. This is an important lesson for those in mainstream society who claim to value life above all else as something that should be protected and treated with dignity and respect. Many of today's environmental activist movements take some of their cues from the Native American concept of the earth and how one should treat all that is in it or on it.

Modern-day earth science and biology classes teach a definition of life that differs from the one offered by Native American tradition. Schools teach that some things are alive and others are not. Native Americans believe that everything is alive and should therefore be treated with the same dignity and respect that we, as only one group of living creatures among many, have come to expect and demand.

This includes every animal, person, rock, plant, tree, element, the earth, the sun, the sky, the moon, and the stars. It includes such simple things as taking the time to observe other living things (all of them, not just certain ones), listening to the lessons offered to us by them, asking permission instead of just taking, and giving thanks not only for what we receive, but for life itself. From a Native American perspective, this is the true meaning of "Thanks-Giving" on a daily basis—it is the true spirit of life.

Impact on the Art World

For early Native Americans, the idea of art was mixed deeply with the worlds of the spirit and of nature. Their depictions of the world around

Creative force
Sherman Alexie is one of a number of Native American artists who are using fiction and film to explore life in their communities today.

them are preserved in some rare cases as cave paintings. As their tribal societies grew more complex, art became more a part of everyday life, with craftsmen and artists creating everything from beaded clothing to pottery sculptures. Art for arts' sake was not that well-known among Native Americans, but rather functional items had artistic and creative qualities. The kachina dolls of the Navajo were representative of spirits, for instance, but their creation can be seen as a form of artwork.

Like so many Native American contributions, it has only been in the past century that the creative aspects of Native art have been recognized for what they are. The discoveries of archaeologists and ethnologists (scientists who study the past and groups of related people, respectively) have created new interest in the arts and crafts of Native Americans of the past. Numerous museums have been built that feature the baskets, clothing, pottery, and even weapons and toys created centuries ago by Native Americans. Their skills are now seen as art, even though they were mostly created with function in mind.

In 2003, the new National Museum of the American Indian opened in Washington, D.C., as part of the Smithsonian Institution. Art and crafts made by Native Americans past and present are part of the huge collection. Other major museums that feature Native American art include the Heard Museum in Phoenix, the Southwest Museum in Los Angeles, and the Philbrook Museum in Tulsa.

Artists who are not Native American have also been inspired by the designs, forms, and styles of Native American artists to create all sorts of art, from sculpture by Henry Moore to paintings by Jackson Pollock. Native American artists today work in textiles, jewelry, sculpture, woodwork, painting, and more, and their creations are prized by collectors, especially in the Southwest. These Native American artists often incorporate themes and stories from their tribes spiritual beliefs. Much modern Native American art also encompasses aspects of the natural world.

New Age Impact

In the later part of the 20th century, another Native American contribution emerged that dealt more specifically with faith. During the 1960s, a wider cultural interest in alternative lifestyles, sometimes involving the use of substances such as peyote (see page 47), drew more people to Native American spiritual beliefs. Some Native spiritual leaders created ways for people who are not Native Americans to take part in these ceremonies and to learn more about Native American traditions. One example was Vincent LaDuke (1929–1992), known as Sun Bear, whose Bear Tribe welcomed outsiders to its traditional ceremonies (see page 108).

More recently the growing New Age movement, which draws on a wide variety of alternative spiritual paths to help people reach new levels of connection, has used some of the themes of Native American spirituality. The connection to the land, the belief in spirits beyond the "real" world, the interest in visions, are all part of traditional Native American spirituality and are part of the beliefs of many New Age groups, as well.

However, the new interest of what could be called outsiders also raised issues within the Native American community. As J. Gordon Melton notes in his 2000 book *American Religions*, "While welcoming the new positive evaluation of Native American [spirituality] that appeared in the 1970s, as well as the support it offered in attempts to preserve traditional ways among Native American peoples, many saw the appropriation of their teachings by whites…as merely the continuation in a new form of the larger community's subjugation of native peoples."

The good thing about the new attention being paid to Native American contributions in this area, as well as all the areas noted in this chapter, is that with attention comes recognition of who actually made these contributions. The problem can be, as noted, that once a contribution has been made, a people loses some of the control over that contribution.

READ ALL ABOUT IT

For a much more complete look at how Native Americans have helped make the world we live in, see the *Encyclopedia of American Indian Contributions to the World*, by Emory Dean Kooke and Kay Marie Porterfield (2002).

Native American Faith and Society

THE POLITICAL ACTIVISM THAT AROSE AMONG NATIVE AMERICANS during the 1960s (see page 49) has led many Native American communities to a renewed interest in traditional beliefs and values. Across the nation, many tribes are spending more time and effort to bring these values to life, both within their own communities and in the wider world. Ancient rites are being renewed, dances from the old days are being brought back, and a society torn apart by outside forces is slowly turning its eyes to the past to help it rebuild for the future.

Today many tribes, such as the Pawnee, continue cultural activities to revive the old ceremonies. The Navajo, Pueblo, Sioux, and many others have annual Sun Dance or related ceremonies to preserve these traditions and sacred teachings. A number of tribes continue to practice such rites of passage as coming of age ceremonies and vision quests (see page 19). While some of these activities, such as the Cherokee Fall Festival, are open to the public, there are also ceremonies that are restricted to members of the tribe.

Even many Christian churches with large Native American populations today include traditional songs in Native American languages, gatherings around food and worship, and youth activities such as powwows to encourage Native American people to be proud of their identity and heritage.

However, those are rare exceptions. For the most part, unlike some other minority groups, Native American values have remained most influential within their own community. Whereas African-American communities are large enough to spread their values and influence to a wider, dominant European-American culture, Native Americans have not had much impact on the dominant culture. The values they espouse, while in some cases shared by the dominant culture, are not seen as being "created" in any way by Native Americans. In many ways, their struggle to make their voices heard is an echo of the struggle they have faced on so many fronts in the years since Columbus landed in the "New World."

Traditional Education

Education is one area where beliefs and values directly affect Native American society and where the Native peoples themselves continue to have some influence.

In the traditional Native American system of education, cooperation is emphasized without submission, because it is believed that every individual learns in his or her own way. According to traditional beliefs, true learning occurs when people are respected and accepted for who they are and what they uniquely contribute to the circle of life, which consists of the social and natural surroundings. Thinking in terms of family/clan/community rather than in terms of "I/me," many Native American children learn by seeing, doing, and cooperating.

Traditionally, Native American children are respected by the tribal community as young people who come into their potential in their own time, but who are of no less status or importance in the community than adults. Their ideas and opinions are valued in the same way as those of any adult. Therefore, Native American children are accorded the status of adult at a much younger age than young people in other cultures.

Many Native American children are deliberately taught skills and important life lessons, both in the natural surroundings and in the home environment, at an earlier age than are children in many other cultures. Whether indoors or outdoors, each of these experiences begins with careful observation of the surroundings and the skill to be learned.

Openness and patience are considered by Native people as essential for adequately learning any knowledge or skill. Children are

Circle of life
This 17th-century drawing by an unknown artist shows a circular dance performed by Native Americans in the Carolinas.

included in many adult interactions as silent but attentive observers whose responsibility is to absorb everything that is going on, including those things that may not be readily evident. As a result, long periods of observation and time for reflection become necessary, in addition to practicing the skill to be learned.

Children also work with older relatives. These activities often include very little verbal instruction or direction from the older relative, with some room for questions on the part of the child. These relatives correct mistakes calmly and positively. (Often, when Native American children enter a mainstream school environment for the first time, the sometimes harsh judgement of mistakes can harm their self-esteem.)

In many cases, Native American children are also encouraged to test their own skills, unsupervised and alone, as the final step in the learning process. This approach to learning is the basis for a tradition practiced by many Native American tribes called the vision quest (see page 19). By going through a vision quest, the child or adolescent seeks to acquire "spirit power" and knowledge through private self-testing. Following the vision quest experience, the individual (now considered an adult) emerges with the ability to demonstrate newfound knowledge, skills, and awareness for the benefit of his or her community.

However, schooling goes on outside the home and community. For many years, the federal government created "Indian schools" that sought to "civilize" the Native people. These reservation schools taught traditional European subjects in European ways. The poor education that many Native Americans received continues today, unfortunately, because many public schools on reservations are not up to the standard of schools in non-Native American communities. The percentage of Native Americans who attend college is tiny compared to the percentage of other Americans

Increased sovereignty for many Native nations also means increased control over education. In many Native nations and communities across the country, efforts are being made to preserve culture by developing programs both in and outside of the schools to teach young people things such as traditional arts and crafts, Native languages, ceremonies and prayers, songs and chants, and dances. Many of these programs began as remedial efforts at residential youth treatment centers and sobriety programs for all ages. As the success of such programs became evident, their popularity has grown. This is a far cry from efforts only two generations ago by state-mandated, religious-run Indian boarding schools, whose primary objective was to strip Native youth of any cultural foundation.

Traditional Values

For many decades, the Bureau of Indian Affairs, through its agents on reservations, prohibited such traditional and cultural practices as Sun Dances and potlatch (a ceremonial feast and gathering held among Northwest tribes), while allowing the continuing presence of Christian missionaries of many denominations. Since 1934, those policies have changed, and today, such Christian and Catholic groups have allowed—and even encouraged—Native American ceremonial practices as part of their rites. This has resulted in such renewals as the use of kachinas and sacred kivas by the Hopi (see page 18), the pipe ceremonies and Sun Dances of the Pine Ridge, South Dakota, and Lakota Sioux, and many other tribal practices and ceremonies.

The American Indian Religious Freedom Act of 1978 (see page 86) opened the way even further for renewal and continuation of

Native American religious beliefs, languages, and ceremonial and sacred practices.

At the center of these traditional ceremonies are a set of Native American traditional values. The adaptability of Native American peoples and their traditional values has preserved a sacred way of life for their children, and their children's children. From generation to generation, the traditional education of Native American children has provided a sacred pathway along which many generations have walked in harmony and balance. As noted, in other faiths and traditions, the values they espouse (Christian charity or Jewish heritage, for instance) have somewhat melded with the wider American culture. Native American values, however, remain in some ways limited in influence to their own community.

Sometimes this limitation is by choice. A few of the tribes maintain practices solely for their members or for members of their group, in a way they see as more strongly protecting spiritual sacredness. Examples include American Indian Church, the Chehalis tribe in Washington State, and the Indian Shaker Church (see page 22).

Also, teaching by Medicine Men or shamans and elders is still very guarded. But there is more openness to sharing and learning tribal stories and legends, as is done by the Cherokee and Seneca, in community settings. This has resulted in a resurgence of ceremonies, dances, and music such as the Bear, Eagle, Beaver, and other animal dances, as well as teaching Sun Dance activities for greater tribal involvement. Even the unique sharing of a type of sand painting done by the Four Cloud People in a Windday ceremony by the Navajo has preserved a sacred way that is also open for others to better appreciate and respect. For youth, it encourages pride in their identity as Native people to see outsiders so interested in these unique "old ways."

Examples of some tribes that have renewed and integrated traditional values include the Cherokee, Alabama Coushatta, Catawba, Ute, Choctaw, Tunica-Biloxi, Pawnee, Crow, Blackfoot, Pauite, and Sioux. There are also many programs in cultural studies and activities, such as intergenerational and cultural preservation projects. The use of videotapes and CDs has made it much easier to share dances and songs, as well as stories and teachings by elders. The small handheld video cameras used today are much less imposing than earlier huge cameras that often intruded on the storytellers' experience.

The Internet has also helped spread traditional values in schools and communities, and even larger tribal membership groups. These ways of sharing information have also started to help spread Native American ideals beyond the Native community, but they have not yet succeeded on a scale of any size.

Turning Values into Action

Whether the wider culture wants to incorporate their beliefs or not, here are some examples of how modern-day Native American tribes take their long-held values and beliefs and put them into action, both within their own communities and in the wider American community.

Cooperation and Sharing. Many Native American children are accustomed to cooperating and sharing. Whatever belongs to the individual also belongs to one's relations, and vice versa. The idea of seeking group harmony through cooperation and sharing takes precedence above all else. Because of the strong emphasis on interpersonal harmony, many Native American children will go out of their way to avoid the interpersonal conflict that can arise with such things as criticism, interference, arguments, and fights, preferring instead to withdraw either physically or mentally and emotionally to preserve harmony and balance.

Working together
Among the many things that Native Americans share with one another is knowledge, such as in this computer class in 2000 at the Denver Indian Center.

Noninterference. Respecting another person's natural right to self-determination means not interfering with that person's ability to choose, even when it is to keep that person from doing something foolish or dangerous. In Native American tradition, noninterference means caring in a very respectful way. Interfering with the activity of others, by being aggressive, for example, is neither encouraged nor tolerated. In this way, a person ultimately shows respect for oneself and one's community. Tribes have different approaches to putting this value into practice as a community. Some tribes who were very secretive and encouraged noninterference have become more open to outsiders as a way to have their need for self-determination better appreciated. Examples of these include the Seminole, Sioux, and several of the Plains Indian tribes. Other tribes, such as the Waccamaw-Siouan, Choctaw, Lumbee, and Oneida, have created youth activities, festivals, ceremonies, and educational programs to both preserve traditions and share with the general public.

Humility. In the traditional way, one of the greatest challenges in life is to recognize one's place in the universe and to honor this always. Humility is essential to a harmonious way of life, where the emphasis is placed upon relation rather than domination. Individual praise is welcomed if it has been earned, but this praise comes from someone else, and is usually given in the presence of the group. Boasting of one's accomplishments and loud behavior that attracts attention to oneself are discouraged in Native American tradition. Sometimes, a Native American child who is singled out or put on the spot will drop his or her head or eyes as a sign of respect for an honored authority or elder. Every Native American and Alaska Native tribe today continues to teach the value of humility as a strength in the family, clan, and tribe. An example of this family humility in action is the annual berry-picking gathering held by Cow Creek Band in Oregon. After gathering the food, they get together as a group to remember their need for humility as a source of strength for their family and tribe.

Being. The traditional way of life emphasizes a unique sense of "being" rather than "doing." For children raised in the traditional way, the purpose of life calls for attention to the experience of action, rather than the action itself. In other words, it is more important to experience and understand a process in life, rather than to focus on the outcome of the

"Indian Time"

While it might not be considered a traditional value, Native Americans' sense of time can affect how they act both within and outside their community. The mainstream idea of time being a measured process, with careful counts of minutes and hours, and schedules to be met, does not always mesh with how some Native Americans see time.

For example, many Native American children are raised to think in terms of what is happening now, and to be aware of what is taking place all around them.

Consequently, many Native American children are very present-oriented and are accustomed to living mostly in the present. They are not taught to live by the clock, since Mother Earth has her own unique rhythms that signal the beginnings and endings of things. So-called Indian time says that things begin when they are ready, and things end when they are finished.

Many Native American children learn this and other things by watching and listening to the wisdom of their elders. While this often works well within their own community, it can cause problems in the outside world, where careful attention to clocks—in everything from school to the workplace—is more rigidly observed and is considered a virtue.

process. For example, the Waccamaw-Siouan and the Chickahominy tribes created their own Baptist church and community center, built around the ideals of respect and "being," by doing things their own way. The Abenaki in Vermont created a Self-Help Association and use technology to preserve their traditional beliefs in this way of life in both in Canada and the United States.

Keepers of the Wisdom: Native American Elders

Native American elders are honored as highly respected persons due to their lifetime of wisdom acquired through experience. Elders bear an important responsibility for the tribal community by functioning as parents, teachers, community leaders, and spiritual guides. Referring to an elder as grandmother, grandfather, uncle, or aunt is to refer to a very special relationship that exists with that elder through deep respect and admiration.

In the traditional way, elders have responsibility for directing children's attention to the things with which they co-exist (family, community, trees, plants, rocks, animals, elements, the land) and to the meaning of these things. In this way, Native American children develop a heightened level of sensitivity for all the relationships of which they are a part, and which are a part of them, for the circular (cyclical) motion of life, and for the customs and traditions of their people.

Raising a child is considered one of the most important responsibilities with which a person can be blessed. For many Native American tribes, a child is regarded as a sacred gift from the Creator, and therefore as more of a pleasure to care for than an obligation or burden. The participation of aunts, uncles, brothers, sisters, and valued friends in raising and caring for a child therefore adds emphasis to the sense of unity that is reflected in relationships within the community.

In the 1990 book *Reclaiming Youth at Risk* (edited by L.K. Brendtro and others), the story is told of a conversation between a young Native American and his aging grandfather. The young man asks, "Grandfather, what is conversation with the purpose of life?" After a long time in thought, the old man looks up and says, "Grandson, children are the purpose of life. We were once children and someone cared for us, and now it is our time to care."

Honoring the elders
Members of six generations of Vine Wells's family came together at her home on the Prairie Island Reservation in Red Wing, Minnesota, to celebrate her 100th birthday in 2002. They sang traditional songs in her native Dakota language.

The traditional approach to relationships focuses on a sense of connectedness, thankfulness, and the importance of giving back. Many Native American children learn to think of Native American elders as the keepers of the sacred ways, as protectors, mentors, teachers, and support-givers. Meanwhile, Native American elders, whose primary purpose is to care for and guide the children, are reminded of the spirit of playfulness, innocence, and curiosity seen in children. As with so many aspects of Native American spirituality, this is another example of the ongoing circle of life.

Opening Up the Circle

The renewal of ceremonies and traditional activities for nations such as the Lummi, Salish, and Yakima people of Washington State provides an example of how traditional religious and modern peoples come together. Their Seven Drum Religion brings together traditional dances, Indian Shakers, Christians, and other religious groups for ceremonies and mutual respect. This respect for mutual relationships has also opened the ceremonial circle to others, encouraged respect for life's energy in all things, and recognized the importance of environmental conservation and the cycles of nature. In a sense, it is a coming together of the modern ways with the old traditions.

The ceremonies focus on dances, such as the Sun Dance, the Eagle Dance, and the False-Face Dance, as ways to recognize the Great One, the nature of the universal circle that surrounds everyone, and the connection we people have with all things that are our brothers and sisters. These dances teach Native people to ward off unwanted spirits, to find a harmony and wellness in their lives, and to respect their elders and families.

More and more, these once-private ceremonies are being revealed to the public to "open up the circle" to include a wider community. The fact that this opening up is accepted by the wider community shows how much improved—though occasionally still tenuous—relations are between Native Americans and the wider American community.

Traditional Influence on Christian Rites

The influence of Christianity is very apparent on tribal reservations today. The story of how European religion mixes with Native American faiths and society is an ongoing one. Some local churches have been

more accepting of including traditional activities related to ceremonial practices, especially with songs in tribal languages and drumming and rattles for song-chants used with funerals and special youth ceremonies. The renewal of the traditional Sun Dance and the growth of the American Indian Church, as well as the Indian Shakers of Washington State, are examples of new Christian denominations based on traditional spirituality.

Some tribes still worry about the "outsider" influence of Christian churches. There remain memories of earlier policies that cast aside traditional Native American beliefs and imposed Christian ones. However, today there is a greater sensitivity to tribal sacred sites, for instance, and to the use of pipe ceremonies and dances.

Medicine and Healing

Many Native American Medicine Men and Women are skilled herbalists who regularly use more than 200 natural medicines. Medicine Men and Women acted in the same way among early Native Americans as today's psychiatrists, psychologists, and counselors. Their ways of healing are beginning to be considered again by mainstream caregivers as successful alternatives to some modern therapies and treatments.

Much of the medicine prescribed by traditional healers is plant-based. Each tribe and each American region (Southeast, Northeast, Plains, Northwest, Southwest, California, Plateau and Basin, Subarctic, and the Arctic) is unique in the species of plants used for medicinal purposes. The Cherokee in the North and Southeast are well known for their use of plants and natural medicines as tonics and for specific cures.

There are also plants common to all these regions that are recognized from tribe to tribe as an integral part of Indian medicine. Some plants sacred to most tribes include tobacco, sage, corn or Indian corn, and sunflower. Tobacco and sage is used as a sacred smudge (a substance burned to create light smoke) in traditional ceremonies. Tonics and blood-purifying formulas were and are used for strength and energy, especially for the hard work needed to farm for long hours. Some of these plants include burdock, comfrey, goldenseal, Indian root, agrimony, alfalfa, elderberry, sassafras, dandelion, and strawberry.

Plants had other uses and meanings beyond medicine. For instance, some were used as an aid to fishing. Devil's shoestring was used by chewing the root and spitting it on the bait. Sunflower was always planted in facing east to have good crops and to survive the winter. Corn—a special species known as Indian corn—was grown and used in Hopi ceremonies as well as by the Cherokee for the Green Corn Ceremony.

There were many plants with specific healing or curative powers that other Americans learned about from Native Americans, such as goldenseal, also known as yellowroot. Today, goldenseal is still used as a natural antibiotic, antiseptic, and antimicrobial for skin and mouth rashes and to stop or control bleeding. There are similar plants, such as alumroot and wild geranium, that were very necessary in earlier times to stop bleeding when you could not get to a doctor or hospital quickly. There were many snakebite remedies and plants used for insect stings, such as the bark of basswood, pine, and the plants called black or Virginia snakeroot, and bloodroot. Redroot got its name because it was used to prevent blood poisoning, and as a wash for ulcers of the skin and sores.

Native Americans healers believed there is a plant or plants that can be used to help ease every illness or disease of humans or animals. Again, the connection is made between the natural world and the life of human beings. This recognition of a spiritual aspect of illness is another important way that Native American values are being incorporated into the wider culture. Treating the whole person has become a part of more modern medicine. Understanding the spiritual effects of being ill or even of dying are considered more important today, in many ways thanks to the influence of Native American beliefs about the connectedness of mind, body, spirit, and earth.

Constitutional Influence

Finally, some of the ideals and practices of our government were inspired by Native American government practices. These include ideas such as women's suffrage (voting rights, such as the powers given to Iroquois women to veto decisions made by male leaders); the pattern of states within a nation; and the tradition of treating chiefs or leaders as servants of the people rather than their master (representative government).

The Articles of Confederation of 1777, a document that was the forerunner to the U.S. Constitution (ratified in 1789), incorporated principles and practices observed by Benjamin Franklin and other American leaders while studying the system of government used by the League of Five Nations, or the Iroquois League. The *Encyclopedia of American Indian Contributions to the World* notes more than 20 direct similarities between the Iroquois Constitution, created between 1000 and 1400, and the U.S. Constitution. For instance, the Iroquois Constitution provides for equal protections and equal rights for all of the Five Nations that made up the Iroquois Confederacy. The U.S. Constitution provides the same protections for all states of the Union. The Iroquois made their leader the war chief, while the U.S. Congress made the president the commander in chief. The Iroquois said that "rites and festivals of each nation shall remain undisturbed and shall continue as before," while the U.S. Constitution says that "Congress shall make no law respecting an establishment of religion or prohibiting the free exercise thereof...."

Native Americans bring to today's society a wealth of values rooted in their spiritual beliefs. As we saw in chapter 3, they have made many lasting contributions to the culture that are already an integral part of the way we live today. Their impact on society has been less obvious, but it seems to be growing as more people come to understand the deeply-held ideals that bind Native Americans to one another and to the land.

5

American Politics and Native Americans

OPPRESSION AND EXPERIENCES WITH DISCRIMINATION ARE AND continue to be a very real part of the Native American experience in the United States. The interaction of the federal government with Native American nations, tribes, and individuals continues to be touchy and mostly one-sided. The relationship has not been helped by more than 300 years of American pressure on Native Americans to give up their lives, lands, and identities. Although relations have improved in recent decades, the friction of history remains. Several key pieces of national legislation, described here, have had the greatest effect on life among Native Americans. For the most part, positive Native American participation in political life was almost completely absent until recent decades. Instead, American politics dictated the Native American way of life.

The Dawes Act

One of the most far-reaching pieces of legislation, and one whose impact was felt for decades, was the Dawes Act of 1887. The Dawes Act (or General Allotment Act) granted ownership of a 160-acre tract of reservation land to every Native American head of household. During the late 1800s, tribes still controlled nearly 135 million acres of land. The purpose behind this clever

THE RIGHT TO VOTE

For hundreds of years, Native Americans were viewed as a threat or a burden to a flourishing American society. Not only did Native people suffer as a result of policies that took away much of what they had, but they also were not granted equal rights legally under the Constitution. They were not viewed as American citizens.

By the early part of the 20th century, Native Americans were no longer seen as a threat to national expansion. Thus, in 1924 the U.S. citizenship of Native Americans was recognized with the passage of the Citizenship Act. The intent of this legislation was to guarantee full citizenship rights for Native Americans, giving them the right to vote. Prevailing prejudices, however, often made taking advantage of that right and enforcing the law very difficult.

legislation was to force Native Americans to conform to the social and economic structure of white America by disrupting the traditional Native approach of communal landholding, and at the same time, freeing up the surplus land that would be created in the process. The result was seen in the sale of large tracts of Native American lands and the increased poverty of many Native peoples.

By 1934, Native Americans had lost nearly 90 million acres of land through government mishandling and mostly fraudulent sales transactions with non-Native Americans who were hungry for land.

The Indian Religious Crimes Code

The outlawing of Native religions through the Indian Religious Crimes Code passed by Congress in 1889 represented yet another dimension of the cultural onslaught. Once, asked why the Nez Perce had banned missionaries from their lands, Chief Joseph, replied (again from Deloria's 1994 book), "They will teach us to quarrel about God, as Catholics and Protestants do.... We do not want to do that. We may quarrel with men sometimes about things on Earth, but we never quarrel about the Great Spirit. We do not want to learn that."

Missionaries divided up the Native population as if they were slicing up a pie, to determine which denominations would control which geographic regions. This resulted, for the most part, in tribal religions being practiced in secret to avoid persecution. Many Native Americans embraced Christianity, further disrupting the integrity of tribal traditions.

It was not until 1978 that Native Americans were granted religious freedom with the passage of the American Indian Religious Freedom Act, overturning the Indian Religious Crimes Code. This guaranteed Native peoples the constitutional right to practice their traditional religions for the first time in almost a century.

The Relocation Programs

Following World War II, many Native Americans who had either served in the war or worked in factories producing war materials, returned home to reservations where times were hard and jobs were scarce. In the early 1950s, a massive federal program was undertaken to relocate Native Americans on reservations to urban areas such as Chicago, Los Angeles, Denver, San Francisco, St. Louis, Cincinnati, Cleveland, and Dallas.

Another bill
Interior secretary Harold Ickes (seated) signs a 1935 bill that provided for additional self-rule by Native American tribes. The bill was one of a series of steps that tried to remove the federal government's responsibility for Native American affairs.

In what was officially called the Voluntary Relocation Program (later renamed the Employment Assistance Program), recruits were given a one-way bus ticket, temporary low-cost housing, and new clothing.

Given the competition for jobs and the overt racism of the time, many Native Americans were either unable to get jobs in their new homes or worked for very low wages. Although some prospered, many relocated Native Americans, separated from the support of extended family and tribal communities and cut off from ceremonial life, simply became yet another addition to the inner-city poor. Some Native Americans remained in urban centers (where there are still high concentrations of Native people today); others returned home to the reservations or rural areas from which they came.

Self-Determination: Alcatraz and Wounded Knee

Inspired by the African-American leaders of the Civil Rights movement during the 1960s, a new movement was born to defend the rights of Native people, using the motto Red Power. During this time, a generation of Native activists developed a pan-Indian (all tribes) organization called AIM (American Indian Movement), committed to taking direct action that would force the public and the federal government to face the massive failures of policies affecting Native peoples.

On November 19, 1969, more than 200 Native people, calling themselves Indians of All Tribes, landed on Alcatraz Island in San Francisco Bay and claimed it as a spiritual center, university, and social service center. They sarcastically compared the island to most Native American reservations, because Alcatraz had no running water, no good housing, no jobs, and was unfit for cultivation. They occupied the island for a year and a half.

The occupation became a rallying point for AIM—a way to focus national attention on the modern problems faced by Native American people across the country. Groups of Native people aligned with AIM all over the country protested to help various tribes reclaim ancestral homelands, defend hunting and fishing rights, prevent the looting and robbing of Native grave sites, and prevent the mistreatment of Native people in general.

Peace at Wounded Knee

The 1973 Wounded Knee standoff between Native protesters and the federal government was a watershed event in the history of the conflict between the two groups. Here, leaders of the protest offer a peace pipe to a U.S. attorney negotiating with them for an end to the siege.

In 1972, five white men kidnapped Raymond Yellow Thunder, a 51-year-old Lakota man from the Pine Ridge reservation in Nebraska. They stripped him of clothing below the waist, beat him severely, and forced him into an American Legion Hall where a dance was taking place. Yellow Thunder, a veteran himself, was paraded for the amusement of white veterans, and later died from injuries inflicted on him by his assailants.

AIM was outraged at the abuse and murder of Yellow Thunder, and demanded justice from the Human Rights Commission of Nebraska, who refused to consider the complaint. More than 2,000 Native American protesters poured into the town where the murder had taken place, and eventually the five white men responsible for Yellow Thunder's death were charged on lesser counts and tried in a nearby town.

Various episodes of Native people being killed under suspicious circumstances occurred within weeks of the Yellow Thunder murder. Members of AIM descended on Washington, D.C., where they took over the Bureau of Indian Affairs building. They demanded among other things, that a federal law be enacted making it a crime to kill a Native American, even if it had to be created as an amendment to the Endangered Species Act. Although the standoff ended peacefully, following this occupation the mistreatment, abuse, murder, and harassment of Native people around the country increased.

In 1973, a large contingent of AIM occupied Wounded Knee in South Dakota, the site where hundreds of Lakota were massacred in the winter of 1890 (see page 46). The ensuing standoff lasted for two months, when the death of two FBI agents during a shootout led to the conviction of Leonard Peltier for the killings, despite much controversy about the evidence against him (he is still in a federal penitentiary today serving a life sentence).

There were two major outcomes of the Wounded Knee standoff, and both owe a great deal to the huge amount of media coverage the incident received. The first was the passage of a number of pieces of legislation designed to make life for Native people better. The second was a huge surge of interest in traditional Native religions and customs, leading to the revival of such traditions as the Sun Dance among the many Native American nations of the Plains, revival of the Potawatomi Fire-Keeper tradition, and the introduction of the Plains Sweatlodge ceremony as a new religious movement.

Religious Freedom

In 1978, Congress passed and President Jimmy Carter signed the American Indian Religious Freedom Act (AIFRA). The law was intended to formalize and guarantee constitutional protection for Native Americans to practice and exercise their traditional religions. Importantly, for the first time it included the preservation of sacred sites as part of the law. This began an ongoing process among many tribes to protect tribal sites such as burial grounds, ancient villages, and other places from outside development (see more on page 90).

The AIFRA reads, in part, "… it shall be the policy of the United States to protect and preserve for American Native Americans their inherent right to freedom to believe, express, and exercise the traditional religions of the American Native American, Eskimo, Aleut, and Native Hawaiians, including but not limited to access to sites, use and possession of sacred objects, and the freedom to worship through ceremonial and traditional rites."

In 1994, Senator Daniel Inouye of Hawaii introduced legislation that became an important amendment to the 1978 law. The 1994 amendment "specifically protected sacramental use of peyote [see page 47], sacred sites, prisoners' rights, the ceremonial use of eagle feathers and other animal parts." The inclusion of peyote use in this amendment was intended to circumvent a 1990 Supreme Court ruling stating that Native people who used peyote were not exempt from narcotics laws that governed the use of the hallucinogenic substance. The reference to eagle feathers was to help Native peoples avoid penalties for using feathers from endangered animals.

It is perhaps a sign of the still-tenuous relationship between the Native American community and the rest of America that special legislation had to be passed for them to enjoy the same religious freedom that every other faith has always enjoyed under the Constitution.

Gambling

When Americans think of Native Americans in the early days of the 21st century, one of the first things that probably comes to mind is gambling. Since the passage in 1988 of the Native American Gaming Regulatory Act (IGRA), tribes have been allowed to create public casinos offering a variety of types of betting, such as card and dice games, and slot machines.

Getting Organized

Dozens of organizations represent large numbers of Native Americans and work with local and federal agencies to gain new rights for Native Americans and protect the rights they have fought to keep. Here are some of the most prominent:

American Indian Movement (AIM) emerged in the 1960s as a leader in demanding rights and equality for Native Americans. "The movement was founded to turn the attention of Indian people toward a renewal of spirituality which would impart the strength of resolve needed to reverse the ruinous policies of the United States, Canada, and other colonialist governments of Central and South America. At the heart of AIM is a deep spirituality and a belief in the connectedness of all Indian people." (Quoted from its Web site at www.aimovement.org; see page 83 for more on AIM.)

Association on American Indian Affairs (AAIA) works to "promote the welfare of the American Indians, Aleuts, and Eskimos of the United States . . . assist and protect the constitutional rights of these groups; improve health, economic and educational conditions…and support the perpetuation of their cultures," according to their Web site at www.indian-affairs.org.

Indian Law Resource Center has offices in Montana and Washington, D.C. According to its Web site at www.indianlaw.org, it is "dedicated to protecting the right of indigenous peoples to live with dignity and respect according to the ways of their ancestors. Our principal goal is the survival of indigenous peoples, including protection of their land rights, environment, and right to self-determination."

National Congress of American Indians (NCIA) was founded in 1944 and is the oldest and largest tribal government organization in the United States. NCAI serves as a forum for policy development among its membership of more than 250 tribal governments from every region of the country. NCAI's mission is to inform the public and the federal government on tribal self-government, treaty rights, and a broad range of federal policy issues affecting tribal governments.

Native American Rights Fund (NARF) seeks to improve the lives of Native Americans through political means.

Casinos and bingo halls have sprung up like wildfire on Native lands, and in some cases for Native nations they have meant more money in a short period of time—and all the challenges that accompany that new wealth. Estimates of annual revenues for Native casinos are as high as $12 billion.

The popular perception by non-Native people is that Native Americans are getting rich off per capita checks, which are the varying amounts of money distributed to tribal members as corporate partners of tribally-owned casinos and bingo halls. In fact, these per capita amounts for many tribes are small, usually distributed maybe once or twice a year, and in most cases have done little to alleviate the high rates of unemployment and poverty among Native people.

A special report in the December 16, 2002, issue of *Time* magazine presented damaging information about the issue of Native American gambling operations. In the words of reporters Donald Bartlett and James Steele, IGRA "created chaos and a system tailor-made for abuse. It set up a powerless and underfunded watchdog and dispersed oversight responsibilities among a hopeless conflicting hierarchy of…agencies. It created a system so skewed—only a few tribes and their [financial] backers are getting rich—that it has changed the face of Native American country."

IGRA regulates Native American gaming into classes such as traditional social games related to ceremonies, bingo and similar games, and casino-style gaming. It also provides for local gaming commissions working with the individual states to ensure fair competition and employment opportunities, protection from involvement by organized crime, and other considerations that benefit both the states and the tribes. This has provided some protections and regulations, but enforcement remains sketchy. Gaming operations established before these rules went into effect continue to be successful under these regulations, including the Cabazon Band of Mission Indians in California, the Mashantucket Pequoit tribe in Connecticut, and the Eastern Band of Cherokee in North Carolina. The Cherokee are one of the more recent tribes to build and operate a casino and hotel on their reservation.

The positive effects of gaming on reservations and trust lands have included employment opportunities with benefits that extend outside the boundaries of the reservations, improved health and dental benefits for tribe members, and special educational and training programs that reach into the community. Many of these programs provide funding for eldercare facilities, youth activities for alcohol and drug addiction prevention, and cultural activities. For example, in December 2002, the Chumash tribe in central California opened a 10,000-square-foot health facility paid for with profits from its reservation casino.

However, although the gaming industry has become a major source of income and economic development for many Native nations, the challenge at this point is how to maintain that investment and plan for the future so that the growth and the benefit to the people continues.

Following an unfortunate historical pattern, the efforts of government to aid Native Americans has turned out to be the cause of more distress than success. The *Time* article detailed a long list of unfair practices by both Native Americans and non-Natives alike. The question of identity and tribal membership (thus qualifying a person for a share of a tribe's profits) has pitted family members against family members and tribal leaders against their fellow tribal members. In addition, the original idea of the act was to let tribes better use their ancestral lands. However, those lands are, as noted elsewhere, often in remote and inaccessible areas. So tribes have sought through a variety of not-always-above-board means to "create" tribal lands in areas more favorable to casino traffic.

While some tribes are getting rich, notes the *Time* article, "the overwhelming majority of Indians get nothing."

Power in Washington

An additional effect is that the casinos have given Native Americans a new way to gain political power through campaign contributions. Often those who donate money to candidates to help them get elected have a

Our sacred land
Members of the Western Shoshone tribe protested against a proposed nuclear waste dump to be built near Yucca Mountain, Nevada—a site the tribe claims as a sacred place in their faith.

Here are some examples of sacred sites currently threatened or already destroyed by development (listed with their associated tribes). Many of these sites are cornerstones of Native religious traditions.

Badger-Two Medicine, Montana (Blackfoot), threatened by companies wanting to drill for oil and gas

Canyon Mine, Arizona (Havasupai), threatened by uranium mining permitted by the U.S. Forest Service

Medicine Wheel, Wyoming (Arapaho, Blackfoot, Crow, Cheyenne, Lakota, and Shoshone), threatened by proposed measures by the U.S. Forest Service to develop the area as a tourist attraction and promote logging in the vicinity

Celilo Falls, Oregon (Umatilla, Nez Perce, Yakima, and Warm Springs), site was flooded in 1957 by Dalles Dam

Rainbow Natural Bridge, Utah (Navajo, Paiute, and Pueblo), destroyed by completion of the Glen Canyon Dam on the Colorado River in 1963

San Francisco Peaks, Arizona (Apache, Hopi, Navajo, and Zuni), destroyed by the development of the Snow Bowl skiing area

better chance to get their voices heard. The *Time* article gave a figure of $9.5 million donated by tribes during the 2000 presidential election year. The *Los Angeles Times* reported (in a November 5, 2002, article) that in 2002, tribal casinos donated more than $4 million to national political parties and spent more than $15 million on lobbying efforts in Washington, D.C.

California tribes alone have donated more than $42 million to state candidates since 1999. In the *Los Angeles Times* of September 10, 2002, Gregg Jones wrote (in "Tribes Flex Power on Sacred Sites"), "Ignoring California's Native American tribes is not an easy choice for a politician these days. With casino-generated cash rolling in, the tribes are a fast-rising political force, plying [California governor Gray] Davis with millions in campaign contributions and expanding their legislative interests beyond their gambling issues."

Spending money in politics is a way for Native Americans to continue the fight for rights and freedoms, whether those rights are economic, social, or spiritual.

Protecting Sacred Sites

The disrespect given things considered sacred by each tribe was and continues to be a key problem in relations between Native Americans, European settlers, and today's Americans. Traditional Native practices are inseparably bound to the land and natural formations that exist in the geographic location each tribe occupies. Native people have sacred places, and they go to these sacred places to pray, fast, seek visions, conduct ceremonies, receive guidance from spirit guides, and teach young people the traditional ways.

Spraying and logging trees, building dams, fences and roads, mining, hydroelectric plants, urban housing, tourism, and vandalism harm or affect sacred sites. Unfortunately, many of the sacred sites revered by Native people are not on lands that are under their control, but instead are under the control of federal agencies intent on using the land for tourism development, logging, or mining.

Before 1970, development that occurred all over America ignored the sacred sites of all tribes. In 1970, however, President Richard Nixon signed legislation returning sacred land at Blue Lake to the Taos Pueblo people in New Mexico. This was the beginning of a trend toward preserving sacred sites and objects.

In 1988, the Supreme Court ruled that sacred Native American sites should be protected from road construction by the U.S. Forest Service in California. This action reinforced the American Indian Religious Freedom Act of 1978 as a federal policy to protect and to preserve the rights of Native Americans to worship as tribes.

The struggle continues to preserve this heritage. Efforts to develop tourist facilities, to practice logging, and to mine areas of America where earlier Native American tribes put their ancestors to rest have has completely stopped. But other sites continue to be in dispute (see the box on the opposite page). As of late 2002, there were pending court actions on sacred sites in Arizona, Montana, Wyoming, Oklahoma, and South Dakota. Efforts to protect some of these areas were greatly aided by the use of tribal money generated by tribal casinos.

A D.C. chief
Senator Ben Nighthorse Campbell (left) is shown with fellow Senator Daniel Inouye at the 1999 groundbreaking of the Museum of the American Indian in Washington, D.C. Campbell was instrumental in providing funding for the new site, which opened in 2003.

Native Americans in Congress

While Native Americans continue to lobby for more just treatment, they realize the importance of personal representation. Two members of Congress are Native American, and they often have a voice in national policy regarding Native Americans.

In 2002, Colorado senator Ben Nighthorse Campbell (b.1933) was the only Native American in the Senate. A Republican, he is one of 44 chiefs of the Northern Cheyenne tribe. Campbell brings a wide variety of life experiences to his work in the Senate, including a stint in the Air Force, a spot on the 1964 Olympic judo team, a reputation as a top jewelry designer, and work as a horse trainer. Campbell served in the Colorado legislature and the House of Representatives before being elected to the Senate in 1991.

He is on several key committees, including Appropriations, Energy, and Veterans' Affairs. He is the first Native American to be the chairman of the Senate Indian Affairs Committee. In that role, he has played a key role in legislation regarding public lands and their rela-

Time to celebrate

Rep. Brad Carson and his wife Julie speak at a press conference following his election to the House of Representatives from Oklahoma in 2000. In addition to being the only Native American in the House, Carson is also an ordained Baptist minister.

tionship to Native American lands and water rights. Because of the toll taken by fetal alcohol syndrome (alcohol poisoning of the fetus in the womb) among Native Americans, Campbell has helped fund programs to fight it. Finally, he was instrumental in passing legislation that created the National Museum of the American Indian within the Smithsonian Institution, which opened in 2003.

Oklahoma congressman Brad Carson (b.1967) was the only enrolled member of a Native American tribe in the House of Representatives as of 2002. He is a member of the Cherokee Nation. A Democrat, Carson studied in England after college and worked as a lawyer and as a White House Fellow (a special assistant to members of the executive branch) at the Defense Department. He was elected in 2000 to represent Oklahoma in Congress and re-elected in 2002. Carson is vice-chair of the Congressional Native American Caucus, which is a small group of representatives with an interest in Native American affairs.

Campbell and Carson are unique in their national status as Native American politicians. With the growing influence of tribes, thanks to gaming money, and continuing discussion of issues presented in this chapter, experts think one way that tribes can gain more influence is by having other Native Americans join Campbell and Carson in government.

6

Important Native American Leaders

THE LEADERS OF NATIVE AMERICAN TRIBES OFTEN COMBINED spiritual authority with organizational responsibilities. The tribe members looked to these leaders for guidance in following traditional ways, as well as for leadership in dealing with Europeans and Americans. Other leaders were more directly in the spiritual realm; as we saw in chapter 2, the prophets and visionaries from various tribes were held in high esteem and were very influential in many parts of Native American life. The people in this chapter contributed in many ways to the spiritual and cultural life of Native Americans in the years after the first Europeans arrived.

Kateri Tekakwitha (1656–1680)

Born to an Algonquin mother and a Mohawk father, Kateri Tekakwitha became a Christian as a young woman and lived, by all accounts, a holy and virtuous life. After much lobbying by Native American Catholic groups, she was canonized (made a saint) by Pope John Paul II in 1980—the first Native American so honored.

As a child, Tekakwitha survived a bout with smallpox—a disease that killed her parents and brother—although she retained the scars of the disease on her face all her life. She was raised by an uncle who was chief of the

Turtle clan of the Mohawks. She learned about Christianity from Jesuit missionaries who worked with the tribe. Although her family did not approve, she continued her studies of Christianity and remained unmarried, despite the fact that most girls of her tribe married when they were still young. She was baptized in 1676.

As she became more open about her Christianity, Tekakwitha found it difficult to remain in her village and moved into a nearby Christian village run by the Jesuits. There her piety impressed even the priests, and she became well-known among Christian Native Americans for her stories and insights that illuminated the ideas of Christianity.

She died in 1680 of an unnamed disease, at only 24 years old. Her legend grew over time, and she became a symbol of the successful merg-

PRECEDING PAGE
Great chief
Sitting Bull was one of the most important Native American military and spiritual leaders during the volatile 19th century.

Saintly person
This painting of Kateri Tekakwitha was made by Father Claude Chauchetière about 1685. The priest knew and worked with the young woman, who would one day become the first Native American Catholic saint.

ing of Native American tradition and Christian belief. A monument erected near her grave in Fonda, New York, in 1884 still attracts many visitors, and her cause for sainthood grew until the pope's announcement in 1980.

Pontiac (1720?–1769)

A chief of the Ottawa nation, Pontiac led a major war against the British Army in the Northwest, the territory near the Great Lakes and the Ohio River Valley.

As the French and Indian War came to an end in North America, France's former Native allies assumed they would be able to live alongside the British. But Lord Jeffrey Amherst, the British commander, refused to help the Native Americans, as the French had. Adding to their concerns, American settlers were moving west and stealing Native American lands.

In 1762, Pontiac began calling for the Northwest tribes to fight together against the British and Americans. Aiding Pontiac was Neolin (dates unknown), a Delaware Native American who claimed to speak with spirits. The Prophet, as Neolin was called, said the tribes had a religious duty to unite against the Europeans so the Native Americans could live as they had in past. Stirred by this message, many tribes joined Pontiac's effort, including the Chippewa, Huron, Seneca, Kickapoo, and Mingo. The war they launched was later called Pontiac's Rebellion.

In May 1763, Pontiac led an Ottawa assault on Detroit, while his allies successfully attacked other forts and settlements. By winter, however, the Native American alliance started to fall apart. The British spread smallpox among some of the tribes, killing many Native Americans, and Pontiac realized that France was not going to provide any aid. Although some fighting continued, the war basically ended in 1764, and Pontiac made peace with the British in 1766. Three years later, he was assassinated while living in Illinois. Despite his military loss to the British, Pontiac inspired future Native American leaders to seek unity in their struggles against the Europeans.

Tecumseh (1768–1813)

Tecumseh (the name means "panther crossing") was born in 1768 into a family of six brothers and one sister. About the time of Tecumseh's birth, a meteor appeared in the sky, and the Shawnee took it as an omen that Tecumseh was going to become an important leader. His father, a Shawnee chief, was killed when Tecumseh was young, and Tecumseh's mother moved with her people to northern Alabama.

Tecumseh was among the warriors at the Battle of Fallen Timbers in 1794, which led to the 1795 Treaty of Greenville that forced the Shawnee into northwest Ohio. Tecumseh boycotted the negotiations and refused to accept the treaty. He recognized that the settlers pouring into the Ohio Valley seriously threatened the Native American way of life.

Tecumseh developed the concept that the Native Americans were all "children of the same parents" and all owned the land in common. Thus, he said, any sale of land or settlement treaty was invalid unless all the tribes agreed. Tecumseh also realized that an alliance of Ohio tribes would be too small to block the U.S. advance, and was determined to develop an alliance of tribes in both the North and South. He

"...And Grovel to None"

So live your life that the fear of death can never enter your heart. Trouble no one about their religion; respect others in their view, and demand that they respect yours. Love your life, perfect your life, beautify all things in your life. Seek to make your life long and its purpose in the service of your people. Prepare a noble death song for the day when you go over the great divide. Always give a word or a sign of salute when meeting or passing a friend, even a stranger, when in a lonely place. Show respect to all people and grovel to none. When you arise in the morning give thanks for the food and for the joy of living. If you see no reason for giving thanks, the fault lies only in yourself. Abuse no one and no thing, for abuse turns the wise ones to fools and robs the spirit of its vision. When it comes your time to die, be not like those whose hearts are filled with the fear of death, so that when their time comes they weep and pray for a little more time to live their lives over again in a different way. Sing your death song and die like a hero going home.

—Tecumseh

From *Shawnee History*, by Lee Sulzman (1998)

dreamed of an Native American nation stretching from the Appalachian Mountains to the Gulf of Mexico, and traveled extensively for years building the alliance.

By 1808, Ohio was made a state and more and more Americans were moving in. Tecumseh and his brother Tenskwatawa (known as The Shawnee Prophet, see page 100) left Ohio and founded Prophetstown in Indiana, which became the capital of the alliance. The Americans watched Prophetstown grow and became concerned that a Native American uprising was being planned, so soldiers were stationed around the town. In 1811, Tecumseh went on a trip to gather support for the alliance among other Native American nations. He warned his brother not to fight the Americans until he returned, but Tenskwatawa believed he had special powers that would protect warriors in battle, and led the Native Americans against the nearby troops.

The battle that ensued, known as the Battle of Tippecanoe, was a minor one for the Americans. Neither side was victorious. But it was a crushing blow to Tecumseh and his dream. Since Tenskwatawa had promised his followers they would be invincible, the fact that the battle could not be won proved he had no special powers. The alliance dispersed and, when the U.S. Army cautiously approached the battleground the next day, they found it abandoned. When Tecumseh returned in January 1812, his hopes for a grand alliance of the Native American nations were shattered.

The War of 1812, between the United States and the British (who controlled Canada) was coming, and Tecumseh supported the British. He hoped that if the British won, the Native Americans could take back their homeland. When the American general, William Hull, invaded Canada in June, Tecumseh fielded 800 warriors in support of the British. During the Battle of the Thames, near Detroit, Tecumseh was killed at the age of 44.

All accounts agree that Tecumseh died bravely, keeping his warriors in the field after the British had retreated. With him died effective resistance to the U.S. settlement of the Northwest Territory.

Tenskwatawa (1775–1836)

In the earliest years of the new American nation, the man known as The Shawnee Prophet became one of the leaders in the struggle with the expanding European-American population.

As a young man, he was given to boasting and bragging, and became known as Lalawethika, which means "noisemaker." He lived a relatively uneventful life until 1805, when he was thought to have become sick and died. He recovered, however, and said that he had a vision of the afterlife of the Shawnee people.

Taking the name Tenskwatawa, which means "open door," he drew thousands of Native Americans from a wide variety of tribes to his side. Tenskwatawa preached that the visions he had of paradise led him to speak to his people about the lives they were leading. He spoke out against the use of alcohol, which he had enjoyed in his life before his vision, and he preached against violence between tribes. Tenskwatawa said the Master of Life, the creator of all, also created the British settlers, but had not created the Americans. This resentment against American invaders of their homeland led many more people to join his growing religious movement.

In 1809, however, the chances for their success were dimmed with the Treaty of Fort Wayne, which deeded millions of acres of land to the new American nation. Interest in Tenskwatawa's movement faded and many Native Americans turned to his brother Tecumseh as a leader with more interest in political and military campaigns.

The Shawnee Prophet lived in Canada for many years, returning to Kansas in the late 1820s, where he died in 1836.

Sitting Bull (1831–1890)

Sitting Bull (Tatanka Iyotake) was born in the Grand River region of present-day South Dakota. As a young man, he became a leader of the Strong Heart Warrior Society and later he was a distinguished member of the Silent Eaters, a group concerned with tribal welfare. He first went to battle at age 14, in a raid on the Crow, and had his first encounter with American soldiers in June 1863. Widely respected for his bravery and insight, he became head chief of the Lakota Nation in about 1868.

In 1874, an expedition led by General George Armstrong Custer confirmed that gold had been discovered in the Black Hills of Dakota Territory. The area was sacred to many tribes and had been placed off-limits to white settlement by the Fort Laramie Treaty of 1868. But gold-hungry prospectors began a rush to the Black Hills despite this ban. The U.S. government offered to buy the Black Hills, but the Lakota did not agree. The Fort Laramie Treaty was then set aside and the Commissioner of Indian Affairs decreed that all Lakota not settled on reservations by January 31, 1876, would be considered hostile. Sitting Bull and his people refused to move.

In March, as three columns of federal troops moved into the area, Sitting Bull summoned the Lakota, Cheyenne, and Arapaho to his camp on Rosebud Creek in Montana Territory. There he led them in the Sun Dance ritual, offering prayers to Wakan Tanka, their Great Spirit, and slashing his arms 100 times as a sign of sacrifice. During this ceremony, Sitting Bull had a vision in which he saw soldiers falling into the Lakota camp like grasshoppers falling from the sky.

Inspired by this vision, the Oglala Lakota war chief, Crazy Horse, set out for battle with a band of 500 warriors, and on June 17 he surprised the U.S. Army and forced them to retreat at the Battle of the Rosebud. To celebrate this victory, the Lakota moved their camp to the valley of the Little Bighorn River, where they were joined by 3,000 more warriors who had left the reservations to follow Sitting Bull. Here they were attacked on June 25 by the Seventh Cavalry under General Custer, whose badly outnumbered troops rushed the encampment and then made a stand on a nearby ridge. There, as Sitting Bull's vision had predicted, all the soldiers were killed.

Thousands more cavalrymen were sent to the area, and over the next year they relentlessly pursued the Lakota. Many chiefs were forced to surrender. But Sitting Bull remained defiant. In May 1877 he led his band across the border into Canada, beyond the reach of the U.S. Army. In 1881, however, finding it impossible to feed his people when there were so few buffalo left, Sitting Bull finally came south to surrender. He asked for the right to cross back and forth into Canada whenever he wanted, and for a reservation of his own on the Little Missouri River near the Black Hills.

Instead he was sent to Standing Rock Reservation in North and South Dakota. But soon government agents were afraid his presence would inspire another uprising, so he was sent further down the Missouri River to Fort Randall, where he and his followers were held for nearly two years as prisoners of war. Finally, on May 10, 1883, Sitting Bull rejoined his tribe at Standing Rock.

In 1885 Sitting Bull was allowed to leave the reservation to join Buffalo Bill's Wild West Show, earning $50 a week for riding around the arena, in addition to whatever he could charge for his autograph and picture. He stayed with the show only four months.

Returning to Standing Rock, Sitting Bull lived in a cabin on the Grand River, near where he had been born. He refused to live by the rules of the reservation, and continued living with two wives and rejected Christianity. He did, however, send his children to a nearby Christian school because he believed the next generation of Lakota would need to be able to read and write.

Soon after his return, Sitting Bull had another mystical vision, in which a meadowlark landed next to him and told him, "Your own people, Lakotas, will kill you."

In the fall of 1890, a religious movement called the Spirit Dance (see page 46) was gaining popularity among the Lakota. The ceremony promised to rid the land of white people and restore the Native American way of life, and the Lakota at the Pine Ridge and Rosebud Reservations had already adopted it.

At Standing Rock, the authorities feared that Sitting Bull, still revered as a spiritual leader, would join the Spirit Dancers as well, and they sent 43 Lakota policemen to arrest him. On December 15, 1890, the policemen burst into Sitting Bull's cabin and dragged him outside, where his followers were gathering to protect him. In the gunfight that followed, one of the Lakota policemen shot Sitting Bull in the head.

Buffalo Bird Woman (c.1839–1932)

Buffalo Bird Woman (Maxi'diwiac) was born on the Knife River in the Five Villages in the Upper Missouri Valley, where the Mandan and Hidatsa nations lived together. She and her brother, Wolf Chief, were grandchildren of an important Hidatsa elder, the keeper of a sacred medicine bundle—two human skulls wrapped in a blanket, passed along for generations and used throughout Hidatsa history to invoke the help of spirits in war, hunting, and especially in bringing rain for their crops.

In her lifetime, Buffalo Bird Woman experienced the change of her people from life in an earth lodge village to life on a reservation. Generations of Americans have heard her story because of an ethnologist (a person who studies the cultures of various national groups) named Gilbert Livingstone Wilson (1868–1930). Wilson interviewed her extensively, then transcribed her words as she shared her horticultural secrets and the social history and customs of the Hidatsa.

In the book (first published in 1917 as *Agriculture of the Hidatsa Indians: An Indian Interpretation*), Buffalo Bird Woman describes a typical agricultural year, from preparing and planting the fields through cultivating, harvesting, and storing foods. She gives recipes for cooking Hidatsa dishes and explains the stories, songs, and ceremonies that were essential to a bountiful harvest. The voice of Buffalo Bird Woman, as recorded by Wilson, brings to life the villages of the Hidatsa people.

Crazy Horse (1849–1877)

Celebrated for his ferocity in battle, Crazy Horse (Tashunca-uitco) was recognized among his own people as a visionary leader commit-

WORDS FROM THE GARDEN

The book Gilbert Livingstone Wilson wrote is still available under the title *Buffalo Bird Woman's Garden*. Here is a short excerpt from Buffalo Bird Woman's words:

I am an old woman now. The buffaloes and black-tail deer are gone, and our Indian ways are almost gone. Sometimes I find it hard to believe I ever lived them. Sometimes at evening I sit, looking out on the big Missouri. The sun sets, and dusk steals over the water. In the shadows I seem again to see our Indian village, with smoke curling upward from the earth lodges; and in the river's roar I hear the yells of the warriors, the laughter of little children as of old. It is but an old woman's dream. Again, I see but shadows and hear only the roar of the river. Tears come into my eyes. Our Indian life, I know, is gone forever.

A work in progress
A vast sculpture has been taking shape for years in the Black Hills of South Dakota. The figure in the foreground is a small study of what the mountain in the background will someday become: an enormous likeness of the Lakota Sioux leader Crazy Horse.

ted to preserving the traditions and values of the Lakota way of life.

While still a young man, Crazy Horse had already become a legendary warrior. He stole horses from the Crow before he was 13, and led his first war party before turning 20. Crazy Horse earned his reputation among the Lakota not only because of his skill and daring in battle, but also because of his great generosity, his ability as a hunter, and his fierce determination to preserve his people's traditional way of life. He refused, for example, to allow any photographs to be taken of him. And he fought to prevent American encroachment on Lakota lands following the Fort Laramie Treaty of 1868, helping to attack a surveying party sent into the Black Hills by General Custer in 1873.

When the U.S. Government ordered all Lakota groups onto reservations in 1876, Crazy Horse became a leader of the resistance. Closely allied to the Cheyenne through his first marriage to a Cheyenne woman, he gathered a force of 1,200 Oglala and Cheyenne at his village and turned back General George Crook on June 17, 1876, as Crook tried to advance up Rosebud Creek toward Sitting Bull's encampment at Little Bighorn. After this victory, Crazy Horse joined forces with Sitting Bull (see page 101) and on June 25 led his band in the counterattack that destroyed Custer's Seventh Cavalry.

Following the victory at Little Bighorn, Crazy Horse remained in the United States to battle General Nelson Miles as he pursued the Lakota and their allies relentlessly throughout the winter of 1876–77. The constant military harassment, and the rapid disappearance of the buffalo due to deliberate overhunting by the U.S. Army, eventually forced Crazy Horse to surrender on May 6, 1877.

Crazy Horse went to live on the Lakota reservation, but remained an independent spirit. In September 1877, he left the reservation without authorization to take his sick wife to her parents. General Crook ordered him arrested, fearing that Crazy Horse was planning further armed resistance. He was taken to Fort Robinson, Nebraska. When Crazy Horse realized he was being led to a guardhouse, he began to struggle, and while his arms were held by one of the arresting officers, a soldier ran him through with a bayonet.

David Sohappy (1925–1991)

David Sohappy was a Native American fishing rights advocate who went to jail in the 1980s while battling the federal government over restrictions on his Yakama tribe's ability to fish in their ancestral waters in the Pacific Northwest.

Sohappy spent his childhood summers on a plot of land owned by his family along the Columbia River in Washington. (In the Sahaptin language his name, Tucknashut, means "provider." Sohappy is the anglicized spelling of his second name, Souihappie, which means "shoving something under a ledge.") He and his family caught and dried salmon, which they lived on during the winter spent on the nearby reservation.

Although he stopped attending school in the fourth grade, Sohappy served in the U.S. Army and later worked as a mechanic, electrician, and running his family's farm. He continued to follow the traditional ways, fishing for several weeks each year. In 1961, after losing a job in a sawmill, he moved his family to Cook's Landing, a tiny windswept point of land jutting into the Columbia River. There he began to fish most of the year, setting in motion events that would place him in the center of three far-reaching legal battles.

"A VERY GREAT VISION IS NEEDED"

A very great vision is needed and the man who has it must follow it as the eagle seeks the deepest blue of the sky. . . . We preferred hunting to a life of idleness on our reservations. At times we did not get enough to eat and we were not allowed to hunt. All we wanted was peace and to be left alone. Soldiers came and destroyed our villages. Then Long Hair [Custer] came. They say we massacred him, but he would have done the same to us. Our first impulse was to escape but we were so hemmed in we had to fight.

—Crazy Horse

as remembered by Charles A. Eastman. (quoted in *Brown Quarterly*, Volume 2, No 4, Winter 1999)

The federal treaties of the 1850s guaranteed Northwest Native tribes the right to fish at their "usual and accustomed places" outside their reservations. The states of Oregon and Washington, however, tried in the 1960s to control the Native fishing with regulations that generally left tribal fishers with a small share of the salmon that were central to their religion, culture, and diet.

Intensified state enforcement coincided with the Sohappys' move to the river. Sohappy believed that the Creator had placed the fish in the rivers for the Native Americans and that as long as they took only what they needed to survive, the Creator would continue to send the fish. Sohappy paid no attention to federal, state, or tribal rules. He fed an extended family of 40, provided the salmon that are central to the tribal Washat (Seven Drum) religious ceremonies, and conducted ceremonies in his own longhouse.

In the early 1960s state officials began to seize his fishing nets on the grounds that he was fishing in areas that were off-limits to him. Sohappy got more nets and kept fishing. In 1968 the state of Washington arrested him, and Sohappy went to federal court. Eventually, a federal judge ruled that Native Americans should get a fair share of the salmon, which was later defined as half the available fish.

Those rulings led to a vicious backlash against tribal fishing in the area. Native American fishermen were taunted and in some cases physically threatened, and tribal fishing gear was damaged. However, the court rulings also resulted in the tribes gaining a voice in establishing fishing seasons and regulations.

Sohappy continued to fish when he needed to, once again in violation of these new rules. He was arrested in 1982, and, after an extended legal battle through federal and tribal courts, Sohappy was sentenced to five years in prison. The case brought national and international attention, including congressional hearings, to the issue of Native American fishing rights. Sohappy's family continued his fight while he was in prison, garnering support from the United Nations Human Rights commission and from U.S. senators Daniel Inouye and Daniel Evans, but Sohappy and one of his sons spent 20 months in federal prison.

A final ruling in the case came in 1991, five months after Sohappy's death. The ruling gave specific legal recognition to Native American fishing rights, gave Native American tribes a voice in managing the Northwest fisheries, and led the government finally to keep a 1939 promise to the Native peoples of the Columbia River to provide 400 acres of fishing sites destroyed by the creation of the Bonneville (Washington) Dam.

Sohappy's insistence on adhering to the ways of his ancestors brought him into conflict with his own tribal government as well as with state and federal governments. Even those who opposed him realized that his defiant actions were key to the recognition of Native Americans' fishing rights and to pushing the government into fulfilling its long-ignored promise of designated fishing sites. A dignified, almost regal, figure, Sohappy had a natural eloquence that made him a favorite of reporters.

In a statement he made from prison to the Senate Select Committee on Indian Affairs in 1988 (quoted in the Roberta Ulrich's 1999

Native American Christian Clergy

There are Native American clergy at various levels in most major Christian denominations. In an effort to more closely identify with the Native community, the Roman Catholic and the Episcopal Churches have also appointed Native American bishops.

Donald Pelotte (b.1945) is a member of the Blessed Sacrament order of Catholic priests. He was named bishop of Gallup, New Mexico, in 1986. He is descended from members of the Abenaki and Algonquin tribes in Maine and was the first Native American named to that high office. Native Americans represent less than 0.5 percent of the American Catholic community, but Pelotte's work shows that Roman Catholics are working to improve relations.

In a speech he gave in 2000 at a Los Angeles Catholic gathering called Encuentro, he said, "When I was selected by the pope, I knew that my Native American ancestry had much to do with his decision. . . . In my 14 years as bishop, I have worked tirelessly in making it clear that the Church is sorry for past mistakes and actively seeks reconciliation."

In 2002, Carol Gallagher (b.1955) became the first Native American woman to be named a bishop in the Episcopal Church. Her mother was a member of the Cherokee nation, and instilled in Gallagher a deep respect for her heritage. In an article published through the Episcopal News Service on November 16, 2001, she said, "I think one of the obvious firsts [of the election] is the opportunity to talk about what it means to be both a Native American and a Christian."

In *Protestant Faith in America* (another book in the Faith in America series), author J. Gordon Melton notes that, "As a bishop, Gallagher has addressed the spirituality of Native American people as she speaks about Christianity. She emphasizes the importance Native Americans place on keeping a close connection to one's immediate family and one's people."

book *Empty Nets: Indians, Dams and the Columbia River*), Sohappy said, "All these years of arguing with the state, and sometimes with my own tribe, don't mean much if I have to be remembered as a criminal and a dangerous poacher. My struggle has been for all the Native American people who have rights along the Columbia River, for our children and for the natural salmon in the river."

Sun Bear (1929–1992)

Sun Bear founded the Bear Tribe Medicine Society, a 31,000-member community of mostly non-Native Americans who follow a traditional tribal lifestyle. In founding the Bear Tribe, he felt the long-neglected wisdom of indigenous people had much to teach today's technology-oriented society.

Of Ojibwa descent, Sun Bear was born on the White Earth Reservation in Minnesota. Originally, his name was Vincent LaDuke. With the exception of a period during the 1930s when the family worked as migrant farm laborers, he spent most of his early life on the reservation. According to his autobiography, *The Path of Power* (1987), at an early age he began having visions that portended his development as a medicine teacher. He studied with his uncles, who were Medicine Men.

He dropped out of school after the ninth grade, and at age 15 left the reservation. Over the course of the next several years, Sun Bear worked as a baker, construction worker, real estate agent, cook, and wood cutter. He also traveled around the country, studying the practices of other Native American groups, and eventually incorporated what he learned into his own synthesis of Native wisdom.

Hearing that draftees would be treated worse than volunteers, he joined the United States Army in 1952 during the Korean War, but deserted soon after basic training. He eventually settled in Nevada to work with the Reno-Sparks Native American colony in downtown Reno. Several years later, he went to Hollywood to work as an actor. But the FBI finally caught up with him, and he spent six months in prison for leaving the army. Upon his release, he went back to Reno.

In 1961, he began publishing *Many Smokes*, a newspaper that carried national Native American news. The Bear Tribe was initiated in 1966 by Sun Bear and three non-Native American women in Reno. It grew slowly, moved several times over the years, and split more than once over such issues as drug use and marriage practices.

The Bear Tribe focuses on self-reliance, and Sun Bear's apprenticeship programs teach survival skills as well as shamanic techniques. The Tribe sponsors Medicine Wheel gatherings that are popular in New Age circles. The group also publishes *Wildfire* (the successor to *Many Smokes*) and markets a wide variety of books and ceremonial materials. In recent years, Sun Bear has become a popular target of attack by American Indian Movement leaders, who perceive the current New Age interest in traditional Native American religion as a form of cultural imperialism—that is, the taking over by non-Native Americans of traditional Native American ways.

Sun Bear has written a number of books that set out the ideas and philosophy of the Bear Tribe. They explain how the traditional warrior's path leads to a good life, whether it is out in the wilderness or in the middle of a city, how to interpret dreams, and ways of integrating the health of body, mind, and spirit.

Don Valerio Cohaila (date of birth unknown)

Don Valerio Cohaila, who is also known as Freddy, is a *yatiri* (priest or Medicine Man), born in the Khallawaya community, 13,000 feet high in the Andes mountains, on the border of Peru and Bolivia. In 1992, the elders of his community sent him to invite people in North America and Europe to participate in a Condor-Eagle Encounter, to be held in Peru that year, to fulfill an Inca prophecy that states, "When the Condor of the South meets the Eagle of the North and fly together, then it will be the sign that the Children of the Mother Earth are reawakening."

In the following years, Freddy moved to the United States and Mexico, organizing educational gatherings in Peru and Bolivia, and taking part in human rights and environmental campaigns. He is committed to educating people worldwide about the historical and contemporary truths affecting Native peoples everywhere. In March 2002 he held an international gathering in Mexico to commemorate the 10th anniversary of the Condor-Eagle Encounter.

His educational meetings focus on the necessity of indigenous wisdom for human survival in balance with the environment. "I have walked throughout our Mother Earth, learned and seen the greatness of her beauty. Spirits have guided me here now, to share with my brothers and sisters of North America. It will be my honor to welcome you to our work, the fulfilling of the Inca Prophesy," he says on his Web site, www.dreamkeepers.net.

Freddy has also founded The Inti Wayna (Children of the Sun) Foundation to provide an education to children between the ages of eight and 16 years who lack economic recourses. The foundation focuses on children from the Aymara, Quechua, and Amazon regions in South America, and incorporates the ancestral education of the native Aymara, Quechuas, and Amazon peoples with contemporary, technological education.

In a 1991 interview with *Life* magazine (published in the book *More Reflections on the Meaning of Life*), Freddy said, "The Planet Earth is a sentient being that thinks, speaks, feels, breathes, and has a soul, just

Great honor
Wilma Mankiller's work as the first female chief of a major Native American tribe helped her earn the Presidential Medal of Freedom, being given to her here by President Bill Clinton in 1996.

like a man does. The Incan priest, or altomisayo, speaks with the living earth as he speaks with the stars and with the wind and with the sky. He performs rituals that let man experience his natural unity with the universe...."

Wilma Mankiller (b.1945)

The Cherokee Nation is the largest Native American nation in the United States, having a slightly larger population than the Navajo Nation. It is also the first Native American tribe to be led by a female chief.

Wilma Mankiller grew up in California, married, and had children, but was a single mother when she returned to the home of her early childhood near Talequah, Oklahoma, the capital of the Cherokee Nation. While she had lived in San Francisco, she developed a deeper interest in social issues as well as in her Cherokee heritage (her father was full-blooded Cherokee and her mother was of European descent). Then, in 1969, a group of young Native Americans occupied the abandoned Alcatraz prison, which sits on an island in San Francisco Bay (see page 49). The event inspired her to assert herself as a Cherokee.

Mankiller found work with the Cherokee Nation in Oklahoma and established herself as a leader when she helped forge a project that improved housing and brought water to a rural and traditional Cherokee community. She was serving as deputy chief when the nation's chief resigned, and Mankiller inherited the top position in 1985. She won the next election in her own right, and received a landslide vote for her third term.

During her tenure as chief, the Cherokee Nation has enjoyed increases in tribal income and services, an increase in new businesses in eastern Oklahoma, the establishment of a major Job Corps training center, and many other accomplishments. In her 1993 autobiography, *Mankiller: A Chief and Her People*, a Cherokee spiritual leader describes how, when he met her, he recognized her from a vision he had. He realized, "that she, Wilma Mankiller, was going to be chief. . . . She is a special gift. She is somebody special."

7

Winds of Change Blow Across the Land

THE STORY OF NATIVE AMERICAN PEOPLE IN THE UNITED STATES continues to be a somewhat sad one. There remain numerous social and political issues that create continuing problems, challenges, and opportunities. In this chapter, some of the key issues Native Americans will face in the future are discussed briefly.

Identity

Native people are the only ethnic minority group that actually has to prove their cultural identity through blood studies, and carry an "Indian card" to prove they are who they say they are. Native Americans cannot qualify for a variety of government programs unless they can prove that they are indeed Native Americans. For some Native people, this is yet another form of oppression; for others, it is just a normal part of everyday life; and for still others, it is a source of pride in tribal membership.

Native Americans have mixed between tribes for eons, and, for the past 500 years, with people of other races. This has resulted in many generations of mixed-blood Native people. It has been estimated that at least 98 percent of the Native population is tribally mixed, while approximately 75 percent are also racially mixed. These days, the term "full-blood" is used to refer to those Native people who consider themselves to be 100 percent of one tribe. However, in reality, more often than not the term probably has more to do with spiritual and traditional lifestyle than with actual ancestry.

Among the long-term issues for Native Americans is the continuing dilution of their genealogy by intermarriage with non-Natives and the survival of urban Native peoples. Just how Native American heritage is measured causes much division and controversy in Native communities, and in some cases leads to social and economic inequities. Although some tribes have modified their enrollment criteria to incorporate members who possess heritage from more than one tribe, no tribe allows enrollment in more than one tribe. The reality is that some people are going to be excluded who should be included, and some people will be included who should be excluded.

Federal and State Recognition

Federal recognition of American Indians and Alaska Natives is based on historical and governmental relationships involving treaties and contracts made in the past with certain tribes. The key word is tribes; individual Native Americans are recognized as tribal members. Under federal laws (such as the Indian Civil Rights Act of 1968 and related federal acts and amendments), the tribes are considered sovereign, with the federal government having a trust responsibility over them.

Historically, the Indian Appropriations Act of 1871 instructed the Senate and the president not to make any further treaties with tribes, and reservations were established under executive orders directly from the president. Beginning in 1919, Congress looked to the Secretary of the Interior and later to the Bureau of Indian Affairs to deal with the question of which people comprised a tribe.

Authorization under the Indian Reorganization Act of 1934 and subsequent rulings by the United States Supreme Court made it clear that the federal government has a trust responsibility for tribes. The tribes, in turn, continue to have responsibility and authority related to civil actions and the education, health, social, and welfare issues of their members. Individual members of a tribe are also citizens of the United States and enjoy those rights granted to all U.S. citizens.

State recognition is based on tribal organizations located within specific state boundaries, which is based on historical and mutual relationships established by state legislatures or executive actions by state governors. As an example, North Carolina has established the North Carolina Indian Commission, with representation from the state and federally recognized tribes within their jurisdiction. Other states, such as Maine, South Carolina, and Georgia, have recognized tribes within their jurisdiction with commissions or staff in the governor's office or another administrative office to deal with Native concerns.

The continuing struggle of groups of Native Americans to become federally recognized will be one of the key issues in the future. A National Public Radio report in November 2002 noted that more than 200 groups were then vying to gain federal recognition for their tribal status. Gaining this status would allow them many benefits, not least of which is the right to establish casinos on their lands.

Tribal Resources

As of 2002, there were more than 300 federally recognized reservations in the United States totaling approximately 55 million acres; 11 million acres (20 percent) of that total within reservation boundaries are owned by non-Indians. Needless to say, this land provides many nations with an array of resources from which to benefit their people, and also with a number of challenges in how to maintain, protect, or expand that base.

There are 44 million acres in range and grazing land; 5.3 million acres of commercial forest; 2.5 million acres of crop area; 4 percent of U.S. oil and gas reserves; 40 percent of the U.S. uranium deposits; 30 percent of western coal reserves; and $2 billion in trust royalty payments made by the federal government. It is an interesting irony that some of the most desolate reservations to which Native Americans were forced to move have become valuable sources of minerals and other resources.

Religious Freedom

As mentioned earlier, passage of the American Indian Religious Freedom Act of 1978 guaranteed religious freedom for Native people in the United States for the first time in almost a century. However, two U.S. Supreme Court rulings severely limited the religious rights the law was enacted to protect.

First, in the 1988 decision *Lying, Secretary of Agriculture, et al.* v. *Northwest Indian Cemetery Protective Association, et al.,* the Supreme

"THE PEOPLE"

It has been noted by anthropologists, linguists, and Native people themselves that the meaning of most tribal names makes a reference in some form or another to "the people." Here are some examples of what some tribes are called today, and, in parentheses, what they called themselves originally—words which to them mean "the people."

Abenaki (Alnanbai)

Biloxi (Taneks Aya)

Cherokee (Ani Yvwiyv)

Comanche (Nemene)

Mandan (Numakaki)

Navajo (Dine)

Nez Perce (Nimipu)

Pima (A Atam)

Sioux (Lakota)

Going Fishing:
A Treaty Rights Issue

Two controversial examples of treaty rights are found in the debate over the fishing rights of Native people in the Pacific Northwest and the Great Lakes area of Michigan, Minnesota, and Wisconsin. In both instances, a variety of tribes in those areas have resorted to protest fishing trips that defy existing state laws and regulations regarding fishing, but that are in accordance with Indian treaty rights granted by the federal government.

One of the most controversial topics is the whaling rights of tribes in the Pacific Northwest. Strong opposition to the traditional practice of using small boats to hunt and kill whales has come from state agencies, non-Native fishermen, conservationists, and environmentalists, and has added to the strain already placed upon tribes by an increased influx of people, more industry, and more recreation in many of those areas.

Court allowed the U.S. Forest Service to pave a stretch of road through an area that is sacred to the Karok, Yurok, and Tolowa tribes of northern California. This decision was made in spite of the Forest Service's expert witness who concluded that the road would destroy the religion of those three tribes.

Second, in the 1990 case *Employment Division of Oregon* v. *Smith*, the Supreme Court denied Alfred Smith, a Native American drug rehabilitation counselor, unemployment benefits because he had been discharged from his position for "misconduct." Smith had attended a meeting of the Native American Church (see page 47), where he used the hallucinogenic drug peyote during prayer. However, the Court failed to recognize and uphold the use of peyote as an integral part of that Native American spiritual tradition.

So alarmed were both the Native and Judeo-Christian communities that coalitions were formed to restore religious freedoms through legislative means. Those efforts continue to this day, with one success being the amendment to the Act that was signed into law by President Bill Clinton in 1994 (see page 48).

Repatriation and Reburial

Among the many sacred sites disturbed or destroyed by such things as historical research, erosion and flooding, plowing, urban development, roads, land-clearing, logging, and vandalism (see page 90) have been the ancient graves of Native people. Perhaps worst of all has been the desecration of Native graves by vandals seeking to loot objects valued on national and international markets.

Grave desecration and looting of Native graves reached its peak in the 1980s. Outraged by such disregard for and violation of sacred areas, Native American nations demanded the immediate return of all that was rightfully theirs, including skeletal remains, burial goods, and sacred objects. In the end, Native people have persevered through the

passage of critical legislation that now protects Native grave sites from looting and provides Native people with legal means for reclaiming both remains and sacred objects.

States such as North Carolina have passed legislation to protect Native American rights of sacred and burial sites that are uncovered in the state, under the Indian Religious Freedom Act of 1978 and legislation related to archaeological finds. There is a stringent process that must be followed to ensure that just remedies are applied. Many of the remains and objects have been ceremonially returned to their original sites, when possible, under the careful guidance and blessing of tribal elders and Medicine people. Efforts continue by a number of tribes and tribal advocacy groups to return all remains and sacred objects to the Native nations from whom they were taken.

Indian Mascots

A constant source of controversy between Native peoples and non-Natives has been sports mascots. Professional, college, and high school sports teams across the country have been challenged to do away with stereotypical, racist images of Native people as mascots. Prominent examples include baseball's Atlanta Braves and Cleveland Indians; football's Washington Redskins; and college sports' Florida State University Seminoles.

For the most part, these images tend to fall into one of two categories: the hostile, warlike Indian; or the dopey, clown-like figure with headdress, big nose, red skin, big lips, and other stereotypical features. Native people in many places have become increasingly outspoken, demanding the same respect both socially and legally that is paid to other cultural and racial groups in the United States.

The most well-known controversy came in 1995 when the Atlanta Braves reached the World Series and several protests were staged outside stadiums where the games were played.

The National Football League's Washington Redskins are annually assailed by protesters to change their team's name, but longstanding tradition has made these efforts difficult and there is little prospect for a change at that level. However, many colleges, such as St. John's University in New York (which changed its name from the Redmen to the Red Storm), and high schools have changed their names to reflect a renewed sensitivity.

Cultural Preservation

There have been very positive advances in cultural preservation since the passage of the Indian Civil Rights Act of 1968 (which settled some sovereignty and jurisdiction issues), the Indian Education Act of 1972 (which provides funding to help educators learn how to better serve Native American and Alaska Native students), the Indian Religious Freedom Act of 1978 (which protects the practice of Native American religions), and similar legislation in many states. While many issues remain regarding how federal and state governments deal with Native Americans, tribes are preserving their cultural heritage, traditions, and language in many ways through family and community programs. Almost every tribe has some type of program in education, health, community, and religious activities to encourage pride in and preservation of their tribal traditions.

Although it is evident that Native people still face many difficulties, many of which originated in the cultural genocide of past decades and which continue the cycle of oppression and poverty faced by Native people today, winds of change have blown across the land. With the surge in cultural pride, one of the biggest challenges for Native people today is to eliminate infighting among themselves and find a common vision that will carry the people safely and successfully into the future generations.

GLOSSARY

chief The elected leader and official of a Native American tribe.

circle of life The general belief among traditional Native Americans that all life is part of a wider circle, that every aspect of the natural world has an impact on every other part.

clan A group of families that belong to a single tribe with a common kinship based on traditional beliefs and practices within a tribe.

coming of age The onset of puberty, usually when a person is 11 to 14 years old. This is the age that, in some tribes, signals certain ceremonies that welcome the young person into adulthood.

hallucinogenic Any drug or other substance that produces hallucinations, which are things, images, colors, or shapes a person "sees" that are not visible to others. Peyote, used in some Native religious ceremonies, is an hallucinogenic drug.

Indian A person who is eligible and recognized as a member of a Native American tribe. The person is of Native American descent and meets membership requirements as an enrolled member of a specific tribe or tribal organization.

Itse Selu (Green Corn Ceremony) A ceremony traditionally held by Cherokee people when the new corn is fit to eat, as a way of giving thanks for *selu* (corn) as the giver of life.

kachina A carved wood figure painted and decorated by the Hopi that represents a sacred tradition and belief, such as causing rain or good fortune.

kiva A sacred place used by the Hopi traditional council for sacred ceremonies.

Manifest Destiny A popular concept in the mid 1800s that territorial expansion of the United States was not only inevitable but divinely ordained.

Medicine Man A tribal person chosen or trained, with special powers and knowledge of the traditions passed down through a specific tribe for healing and ceremonies.

missionary A person sent out by a church to preach, establish missions, and make converts to his or her religion.

nation The largest organizational unit of Native Americans, often composed of several tribes.

nomadic A way of life in which people have no permanent home but move about constantly.

peyote A small, spineless, turnip-shaped cactus, native to Mexico and the southwestern United States that produces some hallucinogenic effects when eaten. It is used in some Native American ceremonies.

potlatch A ceremonial feast and gathering held among Northwest tribes.

powwows A social gathering of individual tribes or groups of tribes that is held periodically.

prospectors Miners who search for gold and other valuables.

psychedelic Anything that causes extreme changes in the conscious mind.

repatriation A decision by the federal government to return land back to a Native American tribe that was taken by force or treaty in earlier years.

reservation Land set aside and held in trust by the federal government for Native American nations who are federally recognized by treaty.

sentient Capable of feeling or consciousness.

shaman A word derived from the Tungusic language of Siberia, which refers to a spiritual or religious healer; often used to refer to a tribal person such as a Medicine Man or Medicine Woman who is chosen or trained to practice traditional spirituality passed down by a Native American tribe.

siege   The encirclement of a fortified place by an enemy intent on taking control of it.

smallpox   A dangerous, infectious disease caused by a virus and marked by high fever and skin blotches and rashes. It was especially disastrous to earlier Native American tribes that did not have immunity to European diseases.

spirits   Native American traditional belief holds that all living things, from animals to plants to people, have spirits, and that those spirits survive in some form after death. They believe human spirits can often communicate with living people in meaningful ways or to deliver important messages.

sovereignty   The right and practice of a tribe to govern itself and its members—a right protected by federal law and legislative action by Congress.

sweatlodge   A lodge built in the ground with a closure of wood and animal hides. Hot rocks and steam produce a high quantity of sweat in visitors. In traditional practice, the sweatlodge is used for purification and healing.

tepee   A cone-shaped tent, traditionally made of wooden poles and and animal skins, and used especially by the Plains tribes.

totem pole   A memorial object among tribes of the Northwest, it takes the form of a large tree trunk carved and painted with faces and figures.

treaty   In this case, a formal agreement between an Indian tribe or tribes and the U.S. government, giving federally recognized tribes sovereign powers and authorities.

tribe   Also known as band or nation; a Native American organized group with shared history and traditions that represents its members through formal recognition by both the community and by the federal or state government.

vision quest   The ceremonial seeking of spiritual guidance and purpose, often used as an initiation into adulthood in many tribal traditions. A youth is sent into the wilderness alone, without food or water, in search of a personal guardian spirit, usually revealed to him or her in a dream.

Wakan Tanka   A Lakota word referring to the "Great Mystery" of how the world was created.

TIME LINE

c. 10,000-30,000 B.C.E. The ancestors of Native Americans arrive in North America via the Bering Strait land bridge (according to many anthropologists).

c. 300 Various Native peoples settle in the Southwest and begin building societies that will become the Pueblo, Hopi, Zuni, and Navajo, among others.

c. 700 Native peoples begin to settle in the Southeast, eventually becoming the Cherokee, Seminole, and others.

c. 1300 Acoma Pueblo, built in what is now New Mexico, is perhaps the oldest continuously inhabited village in what is now the United States.

1492 Christopher Columbus lands on islands in the West Indies. Thinking he had reached India, he names the indigenous people "Indians."

1545 Spanish soldiers found the first settlement in Florida at St. Augustine.

1620 Pilgrims land near Plymouth, Massachusetts.

1640 Massachusetts's colonists begin efforts to convert local Native Americans to Christianity.

1769 Spanish priest Junipero Serra begins founding missions in California and other Western states.

1803 With the Louisiana Purchase completed, the federal government begins action to move Native Americans from the East to western lands.

1809 Tecumseh begins his effort to unite Midwestern tribes.

1831 The Indian Removal Act forces southeastern tribes to western lands.

1890 The Spirit Dance religion is virtually snuffed out following the Wounded Knee Massacre.

1969 American Indian Movement activists occupy Alcatraz Island in San Francisco Bay.

1973 Activists occupy the site of the Wounded Knee Massacre.

1978 The American Indian Freedom of Religion Act (AIFRA) is passed.

1988 The Indian Gaming Regulatory Act is passed.

1990 The Native American Graves Protection and Repatriation Act is passed, ensuring the return of artifacts and relics from museums to tribal burial sites.

1994 President Bill Clinton signs an amendment to AIFRA legalizing the use of peyote in religious ceremonies, among other things.

RESOURCES

Reading List

Bonvillain, Nancy, *Native Americans and Christianity*. Broomall, Penn.: Chelsea House, 1995.

Hirschfelder, Arlene and Paulette Molin, *Encyclopedia of Native American Religions* (revised edition). New York: Facts On File, 2002.

Martin, Joel, *Native American Religion* (Religion in American Life Series). New York: Oxford University Press, 1999.

Taylor, Colin F. (ed.), *Native American Myths and Legends*. New York: Smithmark Publishers: New York, 1994.

Walker, Paul Robert, *Spiritual Leaders* (Native American Lives). New York: Facts On File, 1994.

Weatherford, Jack, *Native Roots: How the Indians Enriched America*. New York: Crown Publishers, 1991.

Wolfson, Evelyn, *From Abenaki to Zuni: A Dictionary of Native American Tribes*. New York: Walker and Co., 1988.

Resources on the Web

CHIEF Web Site
www.chief.org
CHIEF stands for Christian Hope Indian Eskimo Fellowship. The site contains links to more than 60 Native American Christian groups around the country.

500 Nations
www.500Nations.com
A clearinghouse site for links to most of the tribes' individual Web sites, as well as links to places around the United States that can be visited to learn more about Native American history.

National Museum of the American Indian
www.nmai.si.edu
Scheduled to open in late 2003, this will be part of the Smithsonian Institution in Washington, D.C. The Web site will feature highlights of the collections and many opportunities to learn more about Native American culture, faith, and history.

North American Indian & Indigenous People's Organizations and Associations
www.yvwiiusdinvnohii.net/assoc.html
A list of organizations and groups Native Americans have formed, with links to each group's individual Web site.

INDEX

Note: *Italic* page numbers refer to illustrations.

Abenaki, 74, 107
agriculture
    acreage on reservations, 115
    food crops, 54–55
    harvest celebrations, 17, 55–56
    helping colonists, 38, 53–54
    of the Hidatsa, 103
    importance of corn, 15–17, 18,
        58
    irrigation networks, 26
    non-food plants, 55, 57
Alcatraz Island, Calif., 49–50, *50,*
    84, 111, 122
alcohol, 34, 38, 42, 93, 100
Alexie, Sherman, *63,* 64
Algonquin, 10, 30, 107
Allen, Paula Gunn, 64
American Indian Church, 22, 71,
    77
American Indian Movement
    (AIM), 49, 50, 83–85, 87, 109, 122
American Indian Religious
    Freedom Act (AIRFA)
    amendment of 1994, 48, 66, 116,
        122
    cultural importance, 59, 70
    overturn of Religious Crimes
        Code with, 82
    overview, 86
    Supreme Court cases, 91,
        115–116
Anasazi, 26
ancestors, 12, 18
animals, 10, 11, 12, 14, 57, 58
Apache, 14, 43, 46
archeology, 25, *27,* 63, *117,* 117–118,
    122
art, 15, 18, 62–65, 71
Articles of Confederation of 1777,
    56, 79
Association on American Indian
    Affairs (AAIA), 87

balance, 20, 44, 71, 109
Barboncito, 44
baseball, 57, 60, 118
Battle of Little Bighorn, 45, 102
Battle of the Rosebud, 102
Bear Tribe, 65, 108–109
being, *vs.* action, 73–74

Bender, Charles "Chief," 57
Black Elk, 20, 48
Blackfire, 59
Blackfoot, 14, 90
Black Hawk, 33
Brown, Ellison, 57–58
Bruchac, Joseph, 64
buffalo, 12, 17, 102, 105
Buffalo Bill's Wild West Show, 48,
    102
Buffalo Bird Woman, 103
Bureau of Indian Affairs. *See* U.S.
    Bureau of Indian Affairs
burial sites, 84, 86, 116–118, 122

Cabrillo, Juan, 29
California
    Alcatraz Island, 49–50, *50,* 84,
        111, 122
    Gold Rush, 43
    mission system, 30–32, 33, 43
    relocation policy of 1952, 49,
        82–83
    Supreme Court case over log-
        ging road, 116
Campbell, Sen. Ben Nighthorse,
    91, 92–93
Canada, 30, 100, 101, 102
Carson, Rep. Brad, *92,* 93
Carter, Pres. Jimmy, 86
casinos. *See* gambling
Catholic Church
    Black Elk conversion to, 48
    in colonial times, 30
    Franciscan priests, 28, 30–32,
        32, 43, *45,* 122
    Native American clergy in, 107
    Saint Kateri Tekakwitha, 95–97,
        96
    and the Spanish explorers, 28
    traditional dancing in, 8, 21
ceremonies and rituals. *See also*
    dance
    Deer Rider, 57
    Fall Festival, 57, 67
    Fire-Keeper, 85
    forced secrecy, 82
    Giving Thanks, 55, 56
    Green Corn, 15–16, 59, 78, 120
    in kivas, 18, *19,* 120

    overview, 15
    peyote, *47,* 47–49, *77,* 86, 116
    pre-game, 57
    rites of passage, 18–20, 67, 69–70
    sacred sites for, 43–44, 86, *89,*
        90–91, 117–118
    sand painting, 15, 18, 71
    Soyalangw, 17
    sweatlodge, 9, 85
    Washat (Seven Drum), 106
    weddings, 20, *21*
    Windday, 71
Chauchetière, Father Claude, 96
Cherokee
    Corn Dance Song, 58
    Deer Rider ceremony, 57
    Eagle Dance, 14, 59, 76
    Episcopal bishop, 107
    Fall Festival, 57, 67
    gambling, 88
    Green Corn Festival, 15–16, 59,
        78, 120
    herbal medicine, 78
    Rep. Brad Carson, *92,* 93
    roles of men and women, 20
    Trail of Tears, 35, *36,* 37
    wedding ceremony, 20
    Wilma Mankiller, *110,* 111
Cheyenne, 45–46, *91,* 92–93, 104
Chickasaw, 35, *36*
children. *See also* education
    kachina spirits as teachers, 18
    naming ceremony, 18
    rites of passage to adulthood,
        18–20, 67, 69–70
    traditional view of, 68, 75
Children of the Sun Foundation,
    109–110
Choctaw, 40–41, 42, 73, 119
Christianity
    Black Elk interpretation, 48
    conversion to. *See* conversion;
        missionaries
    Eucharist, 48
    and Handsome Lake, 42
    Native American clergy, 107
    Native American influence on,
        8, 21–23, 47, 67, 70, 76–77
    the role of, 21–23
    today, 8, 72–73, 76–77

Chumash, 26, 88
Church of Jesus Christ of Latter-Day Saints, 44
circle of life, 68, 74, 76
citizenship, 5, 7, 82
civil rights, 49, 82, 113–115
Civil Rights Movement, 49, 83
clan system, 12
Clinton, Pres. Bill, 48, *110,* 116, 122
clothing, 6–7, 57, 63
Coeur d'Alene, *80–81,* 82
Cohaila, Don Valerio, 109–110
colonial times
    conversions, 29–30, 122
    the first Thanksgiving, *52–53,* 54, 55–56
    help from Native Americans, 38, 53–54
    Penn's Treaty, *24–25,* 26
    Pontiac's Rebellion, 97
Columbus, Christopher, 8, 27–28, 122
community life
    effects of activism, 8, 49–50, *50*
    interconnectedness of families, 74–75, 76
    openness to outsiders, 71, 73, 76
    use of traditional values, 72–74
Condor-Eagle Encounter, 109
conflict
    with colonists, 30
    French and Indian War, 30, 97
    Indian Wars, 33, 35, 44–46, 101–102, 104–105
    intertribal, 35, 39, 101, 104
    introduction of guns, 38–39
    mission revolt of 1824, 33
    with settlers, 34, 42, 44, 100, 101
    with U.S. troops in 1973, 50–51
    the value of harmony, 71, 72
conversion, 5, 8
    of children sent to boarding schools, 37
    in colonial times, 29–30
    by early explorers, 21, 29
    by Franciscan priests, 28, 30–32, *32,* 43, *45,* 122
    in frontier times, 33, 37
    in response to Indian Religious Crimes Code, 82
cooking, 54
cooperation and sharing, 72
corn, 15–17, 18, 58, 78
Coronado, Francisco, 28
Crazy Horse, 20, 45, 102, 103–105, *104*
creation stories, 7, 8–9, 10–11, 14
creator, 9–11, 76, 106. *See also* Great Spirit; Wakan Tanka

Crook, Gen. George, 104, 105
Crow, 10–11, 101, 104
cultural aspects
    attempts to "civilize" native peoples, 34, 36–38, 43. *See also* conversion; "Indian Schools"
    attempts to destroy, 35, 49. *See also* relocations
    citizenship in tribe, nation, and U.S., 5, 7, 82
    communal land ownership, 82, 98
    of dance, 58, 71
    diversity of tribes, 7, 9, 22
    education about, 68–72
    effects of environment on, 11–12
    oral tradition, 60–62, 71
    relationship to the world, 62, 74, 76
    revival of tradition, 8, 50, 58–59, 67, 70, 114
    role of elders, 69, 71
    of salmon, 106
    sense of time, 74
    sports and games, 57
    traditional values, 57, 62, 70–74, 75
cultural impact of Native Americans
    art, 64–65
    clothing, 57
    helping colonists, 38, 53–54
    limitations in, 68
    music, 59–60
    New Age movement, 65, 108–109
Custer, Gen. George Armstrong, 45, 101, 102, 104, 105

dance
    Bean Dance, 18
    in Catholic services, 8, 21
    circle of life, *66–67,* 68
    Corn Dance, 58
    cultural importance, 58
    cultural preservation projects, 71
    Eagle Dance, 14, 59, 76
    False-Face, 76
    Feather Dance, 42
    portrayal of kachina spirits, 18
    at powwows, *6–7,* 8, 58
    revival of traditional, 70, 71
    Sun Dance. *See* Sun Dance ceremony
    Thanksgiving Dance, 42
Dawes Act, 81–82
death, 20, 79

de Leon, Poncé, 28
Deloria, Vine, Jr., 35, 64
De Soto, Hernando, 28
disease, 31, 33, 34, 38, 42, 46, 97
Dreamers, 43
Dull Knife, 45–46

Earth, 12, 18, 58, 110
education
    Children of the Sun Foundation, 109–110
    in colonial times, 30
    of colonists by Native Americans, 38, 53–54
    in frontier times, 34
    Indian Education Act, 119
    "Indian Schools," removal from parents, 37–38, *69,* 70
    low quality on reservations, 70
    provided by missionaries, 8, 28
    traditional
        role of elders, 74–76
        sense of time, 74
        survival skills, 56
        through stories, 10, 60–61
        vs. mainstream, 68, 69
        ways of sharing information, 71–72, *72,* 74–76
elders, 69, 71, 73, 74–76
Eliot, John, 30
Encyclopedia of American Indian Contributions to the World, 65, 79
Endangered Species Act, 85, 86
England, 97, 100. *See also* colonial times
environmental aspects
    activities of Don Valerio Cohaila, 109–110
    conservation, 76
    dams, 90, 106
    logging, 90, 91, 115, 116, 117
    mining, 51, 90, 115
    relationship to the world, 62
    threats to sacred sites, 90, 117–118
Episcopal Church, 107
Erdich, Louise, 64
Evans, Sen. Daniel, 106

family life, 74–75, 76
festivals. *See* ceremonies and rituals
fire, 14, 16
First People, 9. *See also* The People
fishing
    rights, 105–108, 116
    techniques, 54, 78

food, 54–55, 56, 106
football, 60, 118
France, 30, 33, 97
Franklin, Benjamin, 26, 56, 79
Freddy. *See* Cohaila, Don Valerio
French and Indian War, 30, 97
frontier times, 33–39

Gaiwiio, 42
Gallagher, Carol, 107
gambling, 51, *80–81,* 82, 86–90, 91,
    115
games. *See* sports and games
genocide, 35, 37, 38. *See also* Indian
    Wars
geography, sacred, 14, 90. *See also*
    sacred sites
Geronimo, 46
Ghost Dance. *See* Spirit Dance
glossary, 120–121
governmental systems, 26, 56, 79
grave desecration. *See* burial
    sites
Great Spirit, 9, 13, 17, 37, 82
Green Corn Festival, 15–16, 59, 78,
    120
guns, 38, 54

Haklyut, Richard, 29
Handsome Lake, 41–42
Harjo, Joy, 64
harmony, 71, 72, 76
Hiacoomes, 29–30
Hidatsa, 103
historical background
    colonial times. *See* colonial
        times
    1800s
        genocide, 35, 37, 38
        Gold Rush, 43
        Indian Wars, 33, 35, 44–46,
            101–102
        loss of Indian Territory,
            33–39
        relocations, 35, *36,* 37, *40–41,*
            42
    first European contact, 7, 8, 21,
        26–28
    French and Indian War, 30, 97
    1950s, relocation policy, 49,
        82–83
    1960s and 1970s, activism, 8,
        49–51, *50*
    Revolutionary times, 33, 34, 42
    Spanish explorers, 28–32, 33
Hopi, 11, 17, 18, 70
House Made of Dawn, 62
humility, 73
hunting, 11, 14, 54

immigrants from Europe, 38
"Indian," use of term, 8, 120, 122
Indian Appropriations Act, 114
Indian Civil Rights Act, 114, 119
Indian Education Act, 119
Indian Gaming Regulatory Act
    (IGRA), 51, 86, 88, 122
Indian Religious Crimes Code, 82
Indian Removal Bill, 35
Indian Reorganization Act, 114
"Indian Schools," 37–38, *69,* 70
Indian Self-Determination and
    Education Assistance Act, 59
Indian Shaker Church, 22, 71, 76,
    77
Indians of All Tribes, 84
Indian Territory, 33–39, 42
"Indian Time," 74
Indian Wars, 33, 35, 44–46, 101–102,
    104–105
Inouye, Sen. Daniel, 86, *91,* 106
Internet, 71, 87, 109, 123
The Inti Wayna, 109–110
Inuit, 11, 58
Iroquois, 26, 41, 56, 79
Iyotake, Tatanka. *See* Sitting Bull

Jackson, Pres. Andrew, 35
Jefferson, Pres. Thomas, 33, 34
jewelry, 57, 64
Joseph, Chief, 43, 82

kachina, 18, *19,* 63, 70, 120
Kenekuk, 43
Khallawaya, 109–110
kiva, 18, 70, 120

LaDuke, Vincent. *See* Sun Bear
Lakota. *See also* Sioux
    Black Elk, 20, 48
    Crazy Horse, 20, 45, 102,
        103–105, *104*
    Sitting Bull, 37, *94–95,* 96,
        101–103, 104–105
    Wakan Tanka, 10, 12, 101, 121
    Wounded Knee. *See* Wounded
        Knee
Lalawethika. *See* Tenskawatawa
land
    communal ownership, 82, 98
    and gambling on reservations,
        51, 89
    poor quality on reservations, 33
    spiritual connection to the, 7,
        33, 34, 44, 90
land, loss of tribal. *See also* reloca-
    tions; reservations
    America as "Ours," 35
    during colonial times, 30

given by the Pope to Spain, 28
and Manifest Destiny, 42–43
through the Dawes Act, 81–82
Wounded Knee. *See* Wounded
    Knee
land bridge from Asia, 8, 25, 122
language
    English words from Native
        American, 62
    forcing children to speak
        English, 37
    number and extinction, 22
    revival, 50, 70
    state names from Native
        American, 31, 56, 62
    words for "The People," 115
    written, 28, 30, 37, 61–62
League of Five Nations. *See*
    Iroquois
legal aid, 87
legal systems, 26
Lincoln, Pres. Abraham, 56
literature, 60–62, *63,* 64
Little Bighorn River battle, 45, 102
logging, 90, 91, 115, 116, 117
Longboat, Tom, 57
The Long Walk, 44
Louisiana Purchase, 33, 122

Mandan, 17, 103
Manifest Destiny, 34, 42–43, 120
Mankiller, Wilma, *110,* 111
mascots and stereotypes, 118
masks, 12, 18
Massasoit, Chief, 56
Matheson, David, *80–81,* 82
Maxi'diwiac, 103
Mayhew, Thomas, Jr. and Sr., 29,
    30
medicinal plants, 77–78
medicine men and women. *See*
    shamans
Metacom, 30
Mexico, 30, 109
migration over the Bering Strait
    land bridge, 8, 25, 122
Miles, Gen. Nelson, 105
Mills, Billy, 58
mining, 51, 90, 115
missionaries. *See also* conversion
    banned by the Nez Percé, 82
    definition, 120
    early, 21, 27
    effects of Indian Religious
        Crimes Code, 82
    Franciscan priests, 28, 30–32,
        32, 33, 43, *45,* 122
    impact, 7–8
    Mormons, 44

missions
    California system of, 28, 29, 30,
        33, *45,* 122
    colonial, 30
    Mormon, 44
Momaday, N. Scott, 62, 64
Mormonism. *See* Church of Jesus
    Christ of Latter-Day Saints
museums, 64, 91, 93, 122
music
    of the Chumash, 26
    cultural preservation projects,
        71
    drums, 58, *61,* 106
    Native American in Christian
        churches, 8, 22, 76
    revival of traditional, 58–59, 70
musicians, 59–60
mythology
    buffalo, 12
    corn, 15
    creation, 7, 8–9, 10–11, 14
    fire, 14
    people in the Middle World, 7, 9
    running, 58
    Before Time, 9

Nakai, R. Carlos, 59–60
National American Rights Fund,
    87
National Congress of American
    Indians, 87
National Museum of the
    American Indian, 64, 91, 93,
    123
Nations
    citizenship, 5, 7
    definition, 120
    number of, 5, 22
    removal of status by Congress,
        45
    sovereignty, 70, 114
Native American Church, 47–48,
    116. *See also* peyote ceremony
Native American Graves
    Protection and Repatriation
    Act, 122
Native Americans
    in the Book of Mormon, 44
    Central and South American,
        26, 55, 109–110
    clergy in Christian denomina-
        tions, 107
    in Congress, 86, *91,* 92–93
    diversity, 7, 9, 22
    genocide, 35, 37, 38
    identity issues, 113–114
    population, 22, 26, 31, 38
    use of term, 8

natural resources on reservation
    land, 115
nature, 11, 12, 56, 62, 74
Navajo, 15, 43, 44, 47, 71
Neihardt, John, 48
Neolin, 97
New Age movement, 65, 108–109
New Mexico, the Long Walk, 44
newspapers, 37, 108, 109
Nez Percé, 43, 45, 82
Nixon, Pres. Richard M., 49, 90
noninterference, 72–73

Ohio. *See* Tecumseh
Ojibwa, 10, 108
O-kee-pa. *See* Sun Dance ceremo-
    ny
Oklahoma, Trail of Tears, 35, *36,*
    37
Olympic Games, 58, 60, 92
oral tradition, 60–62, 71
Ortiz, Simon, 64
Osage, *21*

Pacific Northwest tribes
    culture, 11–12
    fishing rights, 105–108, 116
    gambling, 89–90
    modern religion, 76
    totem poles, 12, *13*
Pelotte, Donald, 107
Penn, William, *24–25,* 26
The People, 9, 115
peyote, 47, 120
peyote ceremony, *47, 77*
    amendment to the AIFRA, 48,
        86, 116, 122
    and the New Age movement, 65
    overview, 47–49
Pilgrims, 29, *52–53,* 54, 55–56, 122
pipe, sacred, 12–13, 70, 77, *84*
plants
    crops. *See* agriculture
    medicinal, 77–78
    non-crop, grown by Native
        Americans, 55, 57
    in pre-game rituals, 57
    sacred, 78. *See also* peyote; pey-
        ote ceremony
Plymouth Plantation, *52–53,* 54, 56
political aspects
    activism, 8, 49–50, *50,* 83–84,
        105–108
    federal and state recognition,
        114–115
    gambling, 51, 89–90, 115
    lobbying, 90
    tribal identity and government
        programs, 113

Polk, Pres. James K., 43
Pontiac, 97
Potawatomi, 85
potlatch, 70, 120
poverty, 82, 83, 87
powwow, *6–7,* 8, 58, 120
prayer, 13, 17–18, 20, 55–57, 70, 77
"Praying Towns," 30
preachers, 29–30
Protestantism, 35, 107
Pueblo, 11, 19, 90, 117
pueblos, 26

racial discrimination, 82, 83, 85,
    118. *See also* genocide; "Indian
    Schools"; land, loss of tribal
Raleigh, Sir Walter, 29
reburial, *117,* 117–118
Red Jacket, 33
religious freedom, 33, 47–48,
    115–116. *See also* American
    Indian Religious Freedom Act
relocations
    Choctaw Removal, *40–41,* 42
    The Long Walk, 44
    and Manifest Destiny, 43
    Sioux, and the Indian Wars, 45
    Trail of Tears, 35, *36,* 37
    to urban areas, 1952 policy, 49,
        82–83
repatriation, *117,* 117–118, 120, 122
reservations
    acreage, 115
    casinos on. *See* gambling
    Dawes Act, 81–82
    definition, 120
    inadequacy of the, 33, 36
    "Indian Schools" on, 37–38, *69,*
        70
    natural resources in, 115
    number of, 115
    resettlement to. *See* relocations
    return to, 83
resources for more information,
    87, 123
respect, 71, 73
Revolutionary times, 33, 34, 42
rituals. *See* ceremonies and ritu-
    als
Roosevelt, Pres. Franklin, 56
running, 57–58, 60

sacred sites, 43–44, 86, *89,* 90–91,
    117–118
salmon, 105–108
sand painting, 15, 18, 71
Seminole, 28, 35
Seneca, 33, 41–42
Sequoyah, 37, 61

Serra, Father Junipero, 30, 122
Seven Drum Religion, 76
Shakers. *See* Indian Shaker
    Church
shamans or Medicine
    Men/Women
    Black Elk, 48
    Buffalo Bird Woman, 103
    definitions, 120–121
    Don Valerio Cohaila, 109–110
    Kenekuk, 43
    the role of, 15, 71, 77–79
    Sun Bear, 108
Shawnee. *See* Tecumseh;
    Tenskawatawa
Shoshone, *77, 89*
Silko, Leslie Marmon, 64
Sioux. *See also* Lakota
    revival of tradition, 70
    role in the Indian Wars, 44, 45
    vision quests, 19–20
    White Buffalo Woman, 12–13
Sitting Bull, 37, *94–95, 96*, 101–103,
    104–105
Skaniadariio. *See* Handsome Lake
slavery, 28, 31
Smith, Joseph, Jr., 44
Smohalla, 43
Sneve, Virginia Driving Hawk, 64
social activism
    of the 1960s and 1970s, 8, 49–51,
       50, 83–84
    for reburial of remains, 117
    for salmon fishing rights,
       105–108
Sohappy, David, 105–108
Spain, 28, 30–32, *32*, 43, *45*, 122
Spirit Dance, 46, 102–103, 122
spirits
    animal-human, 10
    definition, 121
    as guides, 55, 57
    kachina, 18, *19*, 63, 70, 120
    power, 69
    worlds of, 20, 43
sports and games
    athletes, 57–58, *58*, 60
    mascots and stereotypes, 118
    traditional, 56–57, 58
Squanto, 56
Standing Rock, 102, 103
Sun Bear, 65, 108–109
Sun Dance ceremony

led by Sitting Bull, 101
    open to other Americans, 76
    overview, 17–18
    prayer during, 11, 101
    revival, 59, 67, 70, 77
    tribes who practice, 11, *16,* 67,
       70, *77,* 101
sweatlodge, 9, 85, 121

Tashunca-uitco. *See* Crazy Horse
Tecumseh, 33, 97–100, *99, 122*
Tekakwitha, Kateri, 95–97, *96*
Tenskawatawa, 33, 43, 99, 100–101
Thanksgiving, the first, *52–53,* 54,
    55–56
Thorpe, Jim, 57, *58,* 60
Thunder, Florentine Blue, *112–113,*
    114
Thunder, Raymond Yellow, 85
time, 9, 74
time line, 122
totem, 12
totem pole, 12, *13,* 121
Trail of Tears, 35, *36,* 37
treaties
    definition, 121
    and fishing rights, 105–108, 116
    Fort Laramie Treaty, 101, 104
    Penn's Treaty, 26
    Treaty of Fort Wayne, 101
    Treaty of Greenville, 98
tribal unity
    ceremonies to promote, 17
    destruction by gambling, 89
    destruction by 1952 relocations,
       49, 82–83
    historical attempts, 97–100
    importance of continuity, 22
    from political activism, 8,
       49–51, *50*
    use of the peace pipe, 13
tribes
    current and former, 22, 31
    diversity of, 7, 9, 22
    federal and state recognition,
       114–115
    "full blood" people, 113–114
    number at first European con-
       tact, 7, 25
    perception of membership, 5, 7
    sovereignty, 70, 114
    totem pole as historical record,
       12, *13*

U.S. Bureau of Indian Affairs, 35,
    44, 50, 70, 85, 114
U.S. Congress, 45, 86, *91,* 92–93
U.S. Constitution, 56, 79, 82
U.S. Supreme Court, 91, 114,
    115–116

values, traditional, 62, 70–74, 75
Vision Quest, 19–20, 67, 69, 121
visions
    of Black Elk, 48
    of Crazy Horse, 20
    of Handsome Lake, 41–42
    from peyote, 47
    of Sitting Bull, 45, 101, 102
    of Smohalla, 43
    of Sun Bear, 108
    of Tenskwatawa, 100
    of Wovoka, 46
voting rights, 56, 79, 82

Wakan Tanka, 10, 12, 101, 121
Wampanoag, 30, 56
War of 1812, 100
Washani movement, 43
Web. *See* Internet
Wells, Vine, *75*
whaling, 116
White, Father Andrew, 30
White Buffalo Woman, 12–13
Wilson, Gilbert Livingstone,
    103
Wiyot, 43–44
world
    First People to the Center of
       the World, 9
    material and sacred, 18
    Middle, 7, 9
    relationship to the, 62, 74, 76
    spirit, 20, 43
Wounded Knee
    defeat, 46, 48, 122
    reclamation, 50–51, 84, *84,* 85,
       122
Wovoka, 46
writers, 60–62, *63,* 64, 108–109
writing. *See* language, written

Yakima, 105–108. *See also* Indian
    Shaker Church
Youngblood, Mary, 59

Zuni, 9, 11